Dare to Dream

Dare to Dream

A prayer and worship anthology
from around the world

COMPILED AND EDITED

BY GEOFFREY DUNCAN

Fount
An Imprint of HarperCollinsPublishers

For my wife, Pat, and daughters, Jane and Ruth, love and thanks for all your support and encouragement. Have fun as you Dare to Dream.

Fount Paperbacks is an Imprint of
HarperCollins*Religious*
Part of HarperCollins*Publishers*
77–85 Fulham Palace Road, London W6 8JB

First published in Great Britain
in 1995 by Fount Paperbacks

3 5 7 9 10 8 6 4 2

Copyright in this compilation © 1995 Geoffrey Duncan

Geoffrey Duncan asserts the moral right to be
identified as the compiler of this work

A catalogue record for this book is
available from the British Library

0 551 02898–X

Printed and bound in Great Britain by
Caledonian International Book Manufacturing Ltd, Glasgow

Contents

dare to dream

Foreword

Educated in a missionary school in a former British colony, I was brought up with an impossibly romantic and somewhat narrow view of Christian mission in the Third World. My consuming ambition from about the age of ten, I recall, was to grow up and join the Christian Brothers who, in my adolescent eye, were all strapping six-foot Irishmen who bestrode the corridors of our school inspiring fear, respect and not a little affection.

Leaving school and arriving in London to read law a few years later, I was caught up with the radical student movements of the heady sixties. My reading of colonial history exploded the romantic bubble with a vengeance. I discovered that there was another aspect to the squeaky-clean image of Christian mission which had been so carefully fed to me within the cloistered walls of my school. I felt cheated and betrayed and was sorely tempted to make a clean break with the church and institutionalized Christianity.

It was only years later, after completing my studies and returning home, when I started to become acquainted with the rich ecumenical work of the church, that I started feeling comfortable again as a Christian. *Dare to Dream* is an endorsement of this renewed faith. It is a towering testament to the rich tapestry of Christian concerns.

From the hearts of such familiar and famous names as Pope John Paul II, C. S. Lewis, E. E. Schumacher, Maurice Bowra and James Roose-Evans to the anonymous voices of the twelve-year-old slum-dweller and the fourteen-year-old

Vietnamese orphan, these poems, prayers, songs, hymns and passages sing of the deep Christian commitment to and involvement in the burning issues of our times.

> We sing with you
> > the song of the universe
> We dance with you
> > the dance of life.

And so *Dare to Dream* covers the whole gamut of our concerns, from racism to ecology, from women's issues to aboriginal rights, from worship and ritual to refugees, from poverty to political prisoners . . .

In dreams, it is said, responsibilities begin, and this encyclopaedic anthology reminds us time and time again, often in striking metaphor and music, of our duties, responsibilities and obligations as true Christians.

In this age of refugees, homelessness and suspicion of strangers, listen to the testament of Pakiso Tondi in 'The Nazarene':

I came to this world a stranger
For already my grandparents
were made strangers in their own land . . .

I needed something, somebody to hold on to
I needed something, somebody to make me belong
I searched everywhere . . .

Then, the Nazarene saw me weeping
And he said, 'Child, I am on your side.
Who can be against you?'
He identified himself with me
He became black, poor and oppressed.

This is endorsed by Kate Compston's incantation:

Give us hearts of flesh
to grieve our hostility
then grant us laughter

and let us reach out.
Even if we do not see
eye to eye clearly

dare us to open up
our lands, be hospitable
bare us, soul to soul.

But *Dare to Dream* bears witness not only to our responsibilities to our neighbours and each other, but also to plants, animals, trees . . . the very earth we walk on. Edmund Banyard writes:

Holy is the soil we walk on,
Holy everything that grows,
Holy all beneath the surface,
Holy everything that flows.

And there is the haiku-like lament of Laura Braithwaite:

Sadness is an earth with
no sun, a tree with no leaves
and a bird with no song.

Dare to Dream is a holistic collection of not just Christian, but human concerns; and, if anything, there is a surfeit of riches. But this is not an anthology to be read at one sitting, but a treasure-house to be taken down from the shelf and dipped into whenever we feel our commitment wavering. It is one of those rare books which the great Guyanese poet Martin Carter may have envisaged when he wrote:

I have learnt
from books dear friend
of men dreaming and living
and hungering in a room without a light
who could not die since death was far too poor
who did not sleep to dream, but dreamed to change the world!

CECIL RAJENDRA

Editor's Preface

My very sincere thanks to the members of the team who have assisted, aided and abetted me as we have dreamed together about this volume of works from around the world:

Francis Brienen is a staff member of the Council for World Mission (CWM). She comes from the Reformed Churches in the Netherlands and works to facilitate women's and young people's involvement in mission.

Kate Compston is a minister of the United Reformed Church in the UK and is a writer and editor.

Martin Gage lives in Leicester, UK, and formerly worked for Christian Aid.

John Reardon is the General Secretary of the Council of Churches for Britain and Ireland.

Janet Wootton is the Minister of Union Chapel, a Congregational Church in Islington, London, UK. She is the editor of the 1996-98 Prayer Handbook produced by the United Reformed Church in the UK in cooperation with the British partner churches of the CWM European Region.

GEOFFREY DUNCAN

Introduction

Nuclear and toxic wastes are dumped in the Pacific Ocean. Cyclones and floods devastate parts of Bangladesh. Drought, hunger and lack of water continue to cast a shadow over parts of Central and Southern Africa. Earthquakes are a threat in India. Volcanic eruptions in Papua New Guinea destroyed a city and the surrounding area. Poverty is a way of life in downtown Kingston, Jamaica. In rural Jamaica 80% of the people live below the poverty line. The way of life for indigenous peoples is threatened by multi-national organizations. Human rights movements seek to liberate people who are abused and threatened in various countries. Women suffer as a result of male domination in most societies.

These facts, and many more, present a challenge to environmentalists, human rights organizations, construction engineers, development and aid agencies, Christians, people of other faiths, people who do not profess a faith and people who care about other people . . . the list could be continued. Instead read and reflect on some of these challenges and concerns as encountered by the Council for World Mission through the poems, prayers, prose and hymns contained within this anthology.

The concerns are not limited only to churches. More importantly, they are, many, many times over, the concern of individuals within and without the church and of people of no faith who wish to face the issues of the day. They are the concern of non-governmental organizations and other allies which have an interest and concern associated with those of the Council for World Mission. Also, this book will provide creative thinking for people who live their lives and worship other than in the Christian tradition.

The Council for World Mission (CWM), with its partnership of 31 churches in 30 countries, is set in six regions with churches situated in Africa, the Caribbean, Europe, East Asia, South Asia and the Pacific. Each church is either a United Church or the people should be willing to unite with another denomination when the occasion arises. The Council is concerned with interdependence, peace and justice issues, the Bible, evangelism, new concepts of mission, ways to invigorate faith into action, challenging the status quo, ecumenism, ecological concerns and how people are affected by them.

Through this partnership communities and churches are assisted to become self-supporting but to remain within the understanding and practice of interdependence. Although self-support is the goal to be realized, it is hoped that when this is attained they will see their role as supporters of those who will continue to struggle in a variety of ways.

The churches are drawn from the Reformed tradition, some of which were previously a part of the London Missionary Society (LMS), which was established in 1795 by ministers who gathered of their own free will as an interdenominational group with the desire to take the gospel to people overseas. The following declaration was formally incorporated into the Plan and Constitution of the Society:

> As the union of Christians of various denominations in carrying on this great work is a most desirable object, so, to prevent, if possible, any cause of future dissension, it is declared to be a fundamental principle of The Missionary Society that its design is not to send Presbyterianism, Independency, Episcopacy, or any other form of Church Order and Government (about which there may be differences of opinion among serious persons), but the glorious Gospel of the blessed God, to the heathen; and it shall be left (as it ought to be left) to the minds of the persons whom God may call into the fellowship of His

Son from among them to assume for themselves such form of church Government as to them shall appear most agreeable to the Word of God.

They were an ecumenical group who may not have realized that they were before their time. Such was the vision of the London Missionary Society, and so it remains today with the Council for World Mission in that ecumenism is a part of the understanding and practice of the churches involved in partnership.

The journey continued until 1973, when the Council for World Mission was formed, although it was restructured in 1977 to form the CWM which is known today. 1977 marked the end of a missionary era and the beginning of world mission. Between 1795 and 1977 the Colonial Missionary Society (1836), which became the Commonwealth Missionary Society (1956), played its separate role, but merged with the London Missionary Society on 1968, when it became known as the Congregational Council for World Mission (CCWM).

In 1972 the Congregational Church in England and Wales and the Presbyterian Church of England united to become the United Reformed Church. The overseas committee of the former Presbyterian Church and CCWM became known as the Council for World Mission. In 1981 the Churches of Christ united with the United Reformed Church and a similar process occurred with their former overseas department. Since 1977 other churches have been received into partnership.

The former LMS included people such as David Livingstone, Robert Moffatt, Eric Liddell, Alfred Sadd and John Williams among its missionaries. There were stories of heroism, martyrdom and colonialism some of which are not to the pride of the former missionary society. For some readers these names will mean much, but for others, very little, as this anthology is intended to reflect on contemporary issues and to be used in a wide variety of ways in societies around the world.

The movements of missionaries and mission have advanced considerably since the days of the London Missionary Society and the prophetic vision of the founders. The Council for World Mission is prophetic in its role of advancing the concepts of partnership and sharing. This is a role which is being examined and adopted by mission agencies and churches around the world. There are close associations with other ecumenical bodies such as the World Council of Churches and the Pacific Conference of Churches, with a continuing emphasis on ecumenical involvement.

The present CWM shares resources. One of these is the sharing of personnel. As an example, this kind of sharing took place when a teacher from the Solomon Islands (a part of the United Church of Papua New Guinea and the Solomon Islands) in the Pacific Region went to work with the Kiribati Protestant Church as a teacher in one of their schools. He believes that we are living in an age when too many people do not know about God and it is the responsibility of Christians, whatever their daily work, to show Christ to others.

In the European Region, a woman minister from the Reformed Churches in the Netherlands works in an inter-faith project in Southall, London. Her husband is a minister of the United Reformed Church in the United Kingdom. Before this appointment they worked with the Church of Bangladesh. This enabled her to bring the experience of working with Asian Christians and people of different cultures and faiths to Southall. The project enables Christians to come to a deeper understanding of their own faith and reflect on their role as Christians in the context of a multi-faith and multi-racial community.

Although the majority of the churches are in the so-called Third World, they are not all, by any manner of means, classified as poor or developing. Those that are, such as Bangladesh and Madagascar, are excellent examples of how people in suffering and struggling situations pull together to help themselves and others. A classic example of this was when the Church of Bangladesh gave sacrificially and sent its partner, the Congregational Christian Church in Samoa, a sum of money to assist them in rebuilding after Cyclone Val. A church in Western Samoa sent financial aid to assist the victims of an Indian earthquake. Taiwan is set in a growing economic situation, as is Korea, but both have problems where cultural differences have to be overcome. The Presbyterian Church in Taiwan is involved in justice issues.

Young people play an important and increasing role in the work of CWM. There are regular workcamps held in the six regions when at least 30 young people drawn from the partner churches attend. They have specific work tasks. They relax and sing together. In addition there is the annual Training in Mission scheme which enables twelve young people to live and work together for one year in the UK and Jamaica. Lives are changed.

CWM aims to assist women to play an increasingly important role in their societies, churches and communities. They are often persecuted, ignored and exploited, sometimes according to their culture. Gradually these prejudices are being overcome and they are beginning to play an important role in their societies and churches.

As partners share their resources, it is possible to make finance available for projects which will help people either in communities or as individuals. Support is being given to the construction of a multi-purpose building to be used as a training centre in a relatively new housing settlement situated between Johannesburg and Pretoria, South Africa. The population exceeds 200,000 with 65% economically active people, but about two thirds are unemployed. Various skills will be taught at the centre.

In New Zealand there is a project to assist the rehabilitation of young Maori offenders who have become alienated from society. Quality care programmes will be instituted to enable them to reach their potential. These are ongoing projects, as such problems cannot be solved quickly.

Communication is very poor in some countries, whether it be by means of travel, the written word or visual processes. Here is a story of determination:

One of the delegates, a women from Myanmar (Burma) showed great determination to attend a consultation in Kuala Lumpur, Malaysia. She lives in a remote part of the Chin Hills in Myanmar where there is no public transport. She had to travel the first 100 miles on foot over the hills, at times with the monsoon around her. This took her about five days after which she was able to travel by three buses for a further five days until she arrived at the capital Rangoon. Then she was able to board a plane for Kuala Lumpur. She had the same lengthy journey on her way home.

This anthology of poems, prayer, prose and hymns drawn from writers around the world is published during the bicentenary year of the London Missionary Society, now the Council for World Mission. In 1995 the Council will celebrate, in a variety of ways, 200 years of work and witness which commenced with the London Missionary Society in 1795. Events will be held in key places in many countries, and these activities will enable people to become more familiar with current and future aspects of the Council.

People will remember the past, including men and women who committed their working lives to being missionaries. There will be time for thanksgiving. However, times have changed and now people can engage in short- and long-term service, neither of which is a commitment for life. People will want to assess the present situation as they look forward with hope.

This anthology aims to meet the needs of these people by supplying material on a variety of subjects drawn from around the world both within the CWM family and from other sources. It is designed for use by people who conduct public worship, as the material will enhance worship and prayer. It focuses on contemporary issues which will be present for years to come. Leaders and ministers will be assisted to highlight concerns which have world-wide implications, thus bringing the world news into the sanctuary so that people can be challenged and moved by faith to take action.

In addition, the material can be used by people for their private devotions, in discussion groups, as they lead or take part in workshops, as a conversation piece over a meal either round a table, on a beach or in a rondavel.

Students will be able to include items to help concentrate the mind upon a particular issue and highlight relevant studies. The anthology will be an important addition to bookshelves around the world and in public libraries.

In offering this anthology to a wide readership, it is hoped that contemporary issues, which help to shape the world, will be taken up by a variety of people. 1995 is a springboard for mission, marked by a celebration. Now is the time to motivate, challenge and act for the future.

GEOFFREY DUNCAN

PART ONE

Dream World

As we dare to dream we know that we live on a beautiful but seriously damaged planet. We catch glimpses of the goodness of creation with its order and rich variety, enough to lift our spirits and lead us to regret. Human violation of earth's integrity threatens all life and is closely mirrored in the aggression that so often characterizes the relationships among human beings. Caring for creation must be accompanied by the search for peace.

Laura Braithwaite's poignant description of sadness as a world without light, beauty or birdsong echoes numerous voices that see in the present pollution of the earth the menacing certainty of eventual disaster. From every continent reports are piling up about environmental damage and destruction. Rachel Carson's terrifying parable of a dead world, with which her prophetic 'Silent Spring' begins, seems to many to be alarmingly close.

Over recent years there has been a growing awareness that caring for the world of nature is not only a God-given responsibility but also a matter of self-interest. So often Christianity was blind to the caring aspects of stewardship, preferring the path of exploitation and the degradation and destruction that resulted from it. There is no doubt that much human progress has been achieved at the expense of nature and much of the damage is irreversible.

This growing realization of human failure has led, on the one hand, to calls like that of the report of the Assembly of the World Council of Churches, Canberra, in 1991 for repentance and conversion, and on the other hand, to renewed appreciation of the beauty and the mystery of creation itself. That appreciation is captured in Tony Burnham's prayer of praise, 'One World', and leads directly to calls for action like that of the young Jews and Christians reported by Barbara Wood, and new statements of faith and commitment like that of Elizabeth Tapia. We all have, in Kate Compston's words, a 'new responsibility'.

The new awareness of environmental responsibility has given a fresh gloss to the biblical vision of ploughshares being forged from the weapons of war. The breakdown of the environment has not only been the result of warfare. The concern for nature, then, closely marries with commitment to peace and reconciliation. This is entirely consistent with the new recognition that human beings are part of God's good creation, and that a holistic concern for the world around us must include the search for peace among the nations and peoples of the world. As we remember the slaughter and destruction of nature and human life which so clearly came together in Hiroshima, we commit ourselves to the future, hoping to experience, in Shirley Erena Murray's words, 'God's true Shalom'.

JOHN REARDON

One World

Loving God we praise you
for giving to the world
fish, birds and animals
and trusting us to name them

Whales that sing beneath the waves
jelly fish and crabs
sticklebacks and sharks
friendly dolphins and porpoise schools
rainbow trout and brilliant neon
halibut and lemon sole
carp and cod and coelacanth

Living God you made them
and these are their names

Thrushes singing
swallows skimming
herons fishing
buzzards hovering
skuas diving
puffins shuffling
robins chatting

Creating God you made them
and these are their names

Elephants and midges
gorillas and gerbils
badgers and hedgehogs
cows, pigs and sheep
kangaroos and kittens
lions and lemurs
crocodiles and monkeys

Enlivening God you made them
and these are their names

Loving God we pray now
for the unity of the breathing world
that we and all your creatures
may live together in harmony and peace
in the name of Jesus

ANTHONY G. BURNHAM
ENGLAND

Holy is the soil we walk on,
Holy everything that grows,
Holy all beneath the surface,
Holy every stream that flows.

EDMUND BANYARD
ENGLAND

The divine presence of the Spirit in creation binds us as human beings together with all created life. We are accountable before God in and to the community of life, an accountability which has been imaged in various ways: as servants, stewards and trustees, as tillers and keepers, as priests of creation, as nurturers, as co-creators. This requires attitudes of compassion and humility, respect and reverence.

FROM SIGNS OF THE SPIRIT
WORLD COUNCIL OF CHURCHES

The destruction of the environment cries out for urgent repentance and conversion. We are beckoned to discover a biblical vision and a new understanding of ourselves and God's creation. The only future foreshadowed by the present crises, both social and ecological, is massive suffering, both human and other than human. 'Giver of Life – Sustain your Creation!' is our prayer; we should pray it without ceasing.

FROM SIGNS OF THE SPIRIT
WORLD COUNCIL OF CHURCHES

Sadness

Sadness is an earth with
no sun, a tree with no leaves
and a bird with no song.

LAURA BRAITHWAITE
ENGLAND

Earth

Old woman, broken backed
and barren
hearted, who
will hold your calloused hands
and tend your sores,
look deep into your
rheumy eyes
and kiss your dribbling mouth
and say 'Stand tall because
I see you youthful,
beautiful, not just
as once you were but
as you are and will be
now I have come home
to give my love'? O who

but I, your driven daughter,
flesh of your flesh, I who
once abandoned you for
other fickle loves, destroying
you to run amok, and pirating
my own heart in that peev-
ish separation? – who
but I must leave
this unbrave newer world –
this glittering babel, which
has crushed, abused and silenced you
until you nearly died –

and ask you
to forgive and hold again
the prodigal returned?

KATE COMPSTON
ENGLAND

The Goodness of God's Purpose

The more scientists discover about the world in which we live and the organization of different forms of life, the more it becomes clear that the generosity and abundance with which God's creation is endowed is a far cry from the meanness of chance, utility and accident. It is now realized that the conditions in which our universe came into being were so extraordinary that, but for split-second timing, it would not have been possible for it to have developed the way it has. The intricacy of the organization of nature speaks of a profound design and mind behind it. There is care at every stage and every step of the creative process. Each new creation follows on from the next, is dependent on the rest of creation. This is particularly noticeable when life is created and each form of life relies on the next for its nourishment and shelter, as well as depending on the inanimate parts of nature – the rain, the sun, the structure of the soil – for its life. We are still remarkably ignorant about this interdependence. We are continually surprised by the effects of our intervention in nature because we fail to take into account the fine balance that keeps the whole extraordinary edifice together, interacting and self-supporting. It is becoming apparent that, as Thomas Merton put it, 'It is a myth that all biological species in their struggle for survival must follow a law of aggression in which the stronger earns the right to exist by violently exterminating all his competition' (*On Peace*).

Evolution as the instrument of God's purpose, rather than as accident, takes on quite a different meaning. Instead of leading us to accept aggression and violence as necessary for survival, it takes us in the opposite direction: we become united to all the strivings and strainings of creation.

Everything we are, we have received through the struggles of thousands of species of living creatures: our eyes with which we observe God's creation, our ears with which we hear God's praises sung by all creation, our bodies with which we move and work and experience pleasures and pain.

BARBARA WOOD

If the Land Could Speak

If the land could speak,
It would speak for us.
It would say, like us, that the years
Have forged the bond of life that ties us together.
It was our labour that made her the land she is
It was her yielding that gave us life.
We and the land are one!

KALINGA, PHILIPPINES

Earth

Then God said, 'Let the earth put forth vegetation:
plants yielding seed, and fruit trees of every kind on earth
that bear fruit with seed in it.' And it was so.

And God said, 'Let the earth bring forth living creatures of every kind . . .' And God saw that it was good.

GENESIS 1:11, 24

Vibrations of pile-drivers
the land shudders from
'developing' to 'developed'
everywhere tower blocks .
and condominiums mushroom
to eclipse a lowering sky.
High rise hotels – more
forbidding than ramparts
of any colonial fortress –
I watch marauding bull-dozers
scalp the distant hills.

(Silence)

I hear of press conferences
of petitions, of signatures
of campaigns and lobbying
but no words will come.
I hear the rain pounding
into desolate spaces
the widowed wind howling
but no words will come.

(Silence)

Prayer

Loving Creator, you did not create the earth for destruction, or
pronounce creation as good, to have us exploit indiscrimi-
nately its resources. You did not give us authority to treat the
earth as real estate, to divide, to barter, to own. Forgive us.

Give us the honesty to recognise our own foolishness;
wisdom to see the partnership between humankind and the
rest of creation; vision to stand in solidarity with those struggling to maintain an ecological balance.

Renew us to live in peace with all creation, that we may say
with you 'It is good!' Amen.

FROM **BECOMING PEACEMAKERS**

Leader	Creator God, breathing your own life into being,
	you gave us the gift of life:
	you placed us on this earth
	with its minerals and waters,
	flowers and fruits,
	living creatures of grace and beauty.
	You gave us the care of the earth.
	Today you call us:
	'Where are you: what have you done?'
	(Silence)
Response	We hide in shame, for we are naked
	We violate the earth and plunder it;
	We refuse to share the earth's resources;
	We seek to own what is not ours, but yours.
	Forgive us, Creator God, and reconcile us to your
	creation.
All	Teach us, Creator God of Love,
	That the earth and all its fullness is yours,
	The world and all who dwell in it.
	Call us yet again to safeguard the gift of life.
	Amen.

CCA WORSHIP, 1991
ASIA

Conflict of Rights

(In 1993 a landowner in an isolated and almost pristine part of South Westland, New Zealand, clear-felled an area of totara trees alongside a scenic route through his forested property. The government was about to enact legislation restricting the logging of native trees for export. The price of timber on the international market had also risen dramatically.)

The *rights of the landholder*, we can easily understand as, being human, we tend to think like he did:
- I own this area of bush which has never given me a financial return.
- I have seen and read of other landowners felling their bush to make big money.
- The land isn't steeply sloping, I could sow it in grass and graze cattle.
- The price of timber continues to climb steeply and I had better act quickly.
- Restrictions on logging native bush are soon to come into force.
- I could travel, upgrade my house, buy a new car . . .
- I don't live in the bush, I don't feel any attachment to it.
- I am angry at attempts by the government in Wellington to restrict my freedom to do what I want with 'my' land.

The *rights of the bush itself*, are not easy to understand because we find it hard to think like a tree!!:
- The bush has been there since the end of the last Ice Age – at least 5,000 years.
- Individual trees have been growing since the first Maori settlement or the signing of the Magna Carta in Britain – close on 800 years.
- Tree roots go deep into the earth, changing the rock into soil, getting moisture and food and anchoring the trees against storm and landslide.
- The trees recycle waste and ultimately return everything (leaves, branches . . .) to the soil.
- The bush is home to birds, insects – a whole complex of

fauna and flora, and is a natural system responding to environmental conditions.
– The bush has survived earthquake, drought and storm but is peculiarly defenceless and mute against the chainsaw and bulldozer.
– The bush has no understanding of monetary value, and offers only peace, tranquillity and an opportunity for men and women as strangers to quietly walk and marvel at its majesty, complexity and age.

Creator God, you work over millennia as well as in each moment of time and you have compassion for all species of life, particularly the most vulnerable; help us to think like a tree and recognise that we are part of nature not apart from nature. Give us a desire to walk in the coolness of the bush, to see the fragile beauty of ground ferns and feel the sponginess of litter-covered soil. Open us to the wisdom of the ages as trees which have lived through hundreds of years slow us down and impart to us a sense of time scales and paces of change vastly longer, slower and more peaceful than the frenetic pace and the uncertainty of monetary value we have imposed on ourselves and our land. Amen.

R. J. EYLES
AOTEAROA NEW ZEALAND

Holy and Hurt

The earth is full of the grandeur of God.
Praise God, thrush and falcon!
Praise him lark and robin!
Praise God, bees and sun-drunk cats!
Praise him orchids and mirk-filled bats!
Praise God all nations!
Let all the people praise God's splendour!

Beneath the feather, the claw,
around the rose, the thorn,
beside the pool, pollution,
above the blue mountain, the cloud:
nature too wounds and is wounded.
Holy is the soil we walk on,
Holy the place we despoil.

God of grandeur and grace,
where we have laid waste your creation,
forgive us.
Where we have hurt and wounded each other,
forgive us.
Where your laws and commandments lie broken,
forgive us.

Forgive us and restore us to your kingdom,
that renouncing
what separates us from you,
we may respond
childlike
to your love,
meeting the demands of faith
on our knees;
not counting the cost
or the pain of discipleship,
as we praise your holy name.

KATE MCILHAGGA
ENGLAND

The Web of Life

Weaver-God, Creator, sets life on the loom,
Draws out threads of colour from primordial gloom.
Wise in designing, in the weaving deft:
      Love and justice joined – the fabric's warp and weft.

Called to be co-weavers, yet we break the thread
And may smash the shuttle and the loom, instead.
Careless and greedy, we deny by theft
      Love and justice joined – the fabric's warp and weft.

Weaver-God, great Spirit, may we see your face
Tapestried in trees, in waves, and winds of space;
Tenderness teach us, lest we be bereft
      Of love and justice joined – the fabric's warp and weft.

Weavers we are called, yet woven too we're born,
For the web is seamless: if we tear, we're torn.
Gently may we live – that fragile Earth be left
      With love and justice joined – the fabric's warp and weft.

(Tune: 'Noel Nouvelet'.)

KATE COMPSTON
ENGLAND

Life or Death

Lord God,
you breathed into us
your pure life-giving,
energising breath
and gave us the care of the earth,
a vast garden of incredible beauty and splendour,
teeming with all forms of life.
You revealed,
through the traditional wisdom
and folk-lore of every people,
the sacredness of all you made,
teaching us not to destroy,
nor covet,
nor hoard material things for their own sake,
but to respect all life,
to share and provide for the whole community,
not forgetting times
when the land itself must rest and be renewed.

You gave us a choice:
life or death.
You challenged us to choose life,
to live in harmony with creation,
that our descendants may live also
and enjoy the wonder of the natural world
but we have chosen death.

You look with sorrow,
calling in the garden,
'What have you done?'
We have taken and plundered trees and land,
tasting the forbidden fruit:
grasping power for its own sake,
wanting to be God,
to own rather than steward
the land you gave to us.

The whole creation cries out for renewal,
for the coming of your kingdom.

MAUREEN EDWARDS
ENGLAND

Environment

In the beginning God created heaven and earth
calling humanity to share with God in caring for that creation.
For this we give thanks to God!

Yet the human struggle to survive,
has been marred by sin,
by selfishness, greed, and the desire for control.
We have treated the world as our property rather than God's
        gift.

The earth cries out in travail
Soil is cut and scarred and blown away
Water and air is polluted
Forests are dwindling and wildlife is in peril
Our way of living puts pressure on the world
and on many other people in the world.

Prayer

Leader: The gentle whisper of the wind rustling the trees
                has stopped
            There are no more trees
            the land is denuded and barren.

Response *Lord, in your mercy, forgive us.*

Leader: The water of life quickly becomes the water of
                death
            Minerals, soil, fertilisers, garbage, sewage, oil,
            disease – all find their way to the water.

Response: *Lord, in your mercy, forgive us.*

Leader:	Trucks, trains, cars, chain saws, earth movers, lawn mowers

replace the muted sounds of nature.
Smoke, ash, chemicals pollute the sky.

Response: *Lord, in your mercy, forgive us.*

Leader: We have tried to banish you from the earth,
ignoring your ever-present spirit, content
with our own happiness, protecting our
soul, forgetting the spirit that ties us
together body and soul, sister and brother,
people and the earth.

Response: *Lord, in your mercy, forgive us.*

COMMISSION FOR MISSION,
UNITING CHURCH IN AUSTRALIA

Prayer

Gracious God,
We praise you for the marvels of your creation,
for plants growing in earth and water.
the life inhabiting lakes and seas,
for all that creeps through the soils and land,
for all creatures in the wetlands and waterways,
for life flying above earth and sea
for the diversity and beauty of your creation
we stand in awe and wonder.

We confess to you, Divine Creator,
that as creatures privileged to have been given the care of
creation,
we have abused your creation
through arrogance, ignorance, and greed;
we are often unaware of how deeply we abuse
the good earth and its marvellous gifts.
We have hurt and extinguished,
we have infected many people by toxic wastes.

We ask your forgiveness.
In sorrow for what we have done we offer repentance.

Help us to have reverence for your creation,
May we learn the wisdom which comes from living in harmony
with you and your creation.
Amen.

COMMISSION FOR MISSION,
UNITING CHURCH IN AUSTRALIA

From anthropocentrism to bio-centrism

Western Christianity places human beings at the centre of the universe. The whole creation was created for the benefit of human beings, who are to dominate over the fish, the birds, and every living thing upon the earth. Creation was condemned and cursed as a result of human sinfulness. But by the grace of God, human beings are offered the possibility of salvation. They, in turn, can save the planet by assuming responsibility as sons and daughters of God.

A contrasting way of understanding the world is by telling the story of the earth and the biosphere. As Thomas Berry has pointed out, the planet earth came into being about ten billion years ago, and life on the planet seven billion years later. Plants appeared about six hundred millions ago, and animals arrived a little later. Human consciousness only came about some two million years ago. The biosphere existed long before us and its complexity has just begun to be understood by biologists in the 20th century. It is arrogant on our part to think that the earth exists solely for our disposal, and that the salvation of the vast and expansive galaxy would depend on just five billion human beings.

Western anthropocentrism creates a God according to the image of human beings: God is king, father, judge and warrior. God is the Lord of history, intervening in human events. On the contrary, the Oriental people and indigenous people who are tied to the soil imagine the divine, the Tao, as silent and non-intrusive. They speak of earth with respect and reverence as the mother who is sustaining and life-affirming. A shift from anthropocentrism to bio-centrism necessitates a change in our way of thinking and speaking about God.

KWOK PUI-LAN
ASIA

Praying for Forgiveness

Forgive us, Father Friend,
because we have betrayed your trust.
You gave into our care planet earth
in all its loveliness and fruitfulness.
We have laid waste the plains;
we have felled the trees of the forest;
we have plundered the ground.
Forgive us.

We have polluted the rivers and seas;
we have filled the air with impurities;
we have ruined the earth with radiation;
we have brought disease where there was health.
Forgive us.

You created the animals and asked us to nurture them.
We have hunted and destroyed countless of your creatures;
for greed and pride we have extinguished whole species;
we have driven mad animals that trusted us
and caused indescribable suffering to sensitive creatures.
Forgive us
and help us by your Holy Spirit
to be better stewards of our planet and its inhabitants.

JOHN JOHANSEN-BERG
ENGLAND

Waste

Not only in ancient ruined cities
but in and around the modern city
are the waste-heaps and garbage of our lives,
picked over by the foxes and the crows
and the human scavengers who make a living there.

Forgive us, Lord, for mentioning
      our rubbish in our prayers.
      We would rather enjoy the fruits of creation
      and forget about the consequences.
Forgive us our polluted water,
      our toxic soil and sulphurous air.
Forgive us all the dumped surpluses,
      the slag heaps and the piles of scrap.

We thank you for the signs of your forgiveness;
for the plants and trees which colonise
even the most unsightly ground;
for the animals and birds who learn to live
in secret places in our urban sprawl
and turn our rubbish to good account.

We thank you for those who deal with our rubbish,
who keep our streets and houses healthy;
who guard us against poisons and radiation,
or who turn our waste into new riches.

We pray for those for whom the rubbish tip
is the only source of food and wealth,
picking through others' leavings in the search
to keep their family alive.

Most generous giver, from whose creation there is enough for all and to
spare, make us wise stewards of the earth's treasure and generous in
our turn to one another.

STEPHEN ORCHARD
ENGLAND

A civilisation ruled almost exclusively by town-dwellers is always in danger of forgetting the basic truth: that if man should win the battle against nature he would find himself on the losing side.

E. F. SCHUMACHER

The Whole Environment

One of the most remarkable experiences I have had is, after walking for miles through Malagasy countryside impoverished by 'slash and burn' agriculture, to enter an area of primary rainforest. It was like walking off a hot city street into a cool air-conditioned hotel – but much more wonderful. Primary rainforest is teeming with life from the tops of tall trees clothed in lichen, epiphytic ferns and orchids down to soil level, thick with decaying leaves and fallen branches. The soil itself may be shallow but the rich mix of roots and humus acts as a sponge during times of torrential rain.

The evolutionary development of Madagascar's flora and fauna has resulted in a high level of endemism. For the size of the country the Malagasy flora is one of the richest in the world. Because so much former vegetation has been destroyed, soil erosion can be seen everywhere, the red soil of Madagascar bleeding into the surrounding ocean. The growing population, 85% of which live in the countryside, places an ever increasing pressure on areas precious for wildlife. People depend upon food they grow themselves, generally relying on traditional methods of agriculture.

PHILIP JONES
WALES/MADAGASCAR

Deforestation

As a result of deforestation around Lake Madden the Panama Canal is silting up and may become operationally useless. As a result of deforestation in the Himalayas, India spends over $1 billion annually on river defences to control seasonal flooding. Throughout the Sahel region of Africa we can see the devastating spiral of natural degradation which follows deforestation. As wood becomes scarce, people burn crop residues and animal dung for cooking and heating, which deprives the already impoverished land of nutrients. Soil fertility drops, crops fail, over-grazed domestic herds reduce grassland, once forest, to desert and people move to other wooded areas, where the process is repeated. When the forests go, it is the people who suffer.

FRIENDS OF THE EARTH

The forest is our livelihood. We have lived here before any of you outsiders came. We fished in clean rivers and hunted in the jungle. We made our sago meat and ate fruit of trees. Our life was not easy but we lived it in content. Now the logging companies turn rivers into muddy streams and the jungle into devastation. The fish cannot survive in dirty rivers and wild animals will not live in devastated forests. You took advantage of our trusting nature and cheated us into unfair deals. By your doing, you have taken away our livelihood and threaten our very lives. We want our ancestral land, the land we live on, back. We can use it in a wiser way. When you come to us, come as guests, with respect.

DECLARATION OF THE PENAN PEOPLE
BORNEO

Singing

It has been the long-enduring testimony of the Church that it only really begins to sing the new song when hope is gone.

PRESBYTERIAN CHURCH, USA

How
can we sing a new song from
the valley of shards?
We are broken vessels
in a fissured land, indeed
we can hear
the parchment earth crack open
beneath our feet even
as we speak.

What
can we do *except*
sing songs of protest, lamentation, hope
from split and bleeding lips
in the valley of splintered dreams?
What, except believe
that earth, like a fragile egg
cracks open to expose
new quiverings of life?

KATE COMPSTON
ENGLAND

Flowers

I have never learnt the names of flowers.
From beginning, my world has been a place
Of pot-holed streets where thick, sluggish gutters race
In slow time, away from garbage heaps and sewers
Past blanched old houses around which cowers
Stagnant earth. There, scarce green thing grew to chase
The dull-grey squalor of sick dust; no trace
Of plant save few sparse weeds; just these, no flowers.

One day they cleared a space and made a park
There in the city's slums; and suddenly
Came stark glory like lightning in the dark,
While perfume and bright petals thundered slowly.
I learnt no names, but hue, shape and scent mark
My mind, even now, with symbols holy.

DENNIS CRAIG
JAMAICA

In October 1982 young Jews and Christians met together to explore the meaning of their faith in the context of today's ecological and environmental crisis. They were addressed by Rabbis and Christian pastors, but much of their time was spent in joint Bible study. In the six days they were together some of them discovered in their own way that while the truth of 'the original commandments' remains unchanged, the law of love shows a new and vital interpretation for today's problems. They united the old and the new in the form of ten ecological commandments:

1. I am the Lord your God who have created heavens and earth. Know that you are my partner in creation; therefore, take care of the air, water, earth, plants and animals, as if they were your brothers and sisters.
2. Know that in giving you life I have given you responsibility, freedom and limited resources.
3. Steal not from the future; honour your children by giving them a chance at longevity.

4. Implant in your children a love of nature.
5. Remember that humanity can use technology, but cannot recreate life that has been destroyed.
6. Set up pressure groups within your community to prevent impending catastrophes.
7. Throw out all arms which cause irreversible destruction to the foundations of life.
8. Be self-disciplined in the small details of your life.
9. Set aside time in your weekly day of rest to be with the world rather than to use the world.
10. Remember that you are not the owner of the land, merely its guardian.

BARBARA WOOD

In this dark world of turmoil,
Christ's light must shine through us.
Let's practise what we preach,
With joyful love and happiness,
For, no matter where we go
This world created by God,
Is ours to make or break.

MONA RIINI, TUHDE TRIBE
AOTEAROA NEW ZEALAND

Earth Credo

I believe in the sacredness of the earth,
>   the integrity of the whole creation
>   and dignity of all peoples and creatures.

I believe in a gracious God who created humankind,
>   male and female in God's image
>   and gave them the gift and responsibility
>   to take care of the earth.
>   *We need to care.*

I believe we human beings have failed God and ourselves.
>   In the name of greed and 'development'
>   we have dominated the earth, degraded people and
>   creatures,
>   destroyed the forests, polluted the air, rivers and seas,
>   and have sacrificed the future of our children.
>   *We need to repent.*

I believe that when we destroy the earth we kill ourselves.
>   We need to preserve and protect the earth,
>   not only for our own survival,
>   but for the sake of our Mother Earth.
>   *The time to change is now.*

I believe we need to change our ways, values,
>   lifestyles and ways of relating with creation.
>   Repent, fast and pray. Consume less . . . waste not.
>   Work for justice and peace.
>   We should not covet our neighbour's timber,
>   butterflies, white sand beaches,
>   nearly extinct animals nor cheap labour.
>   We should not oppress children, indigenous people,
>   women,
>   the homeless, refugees and victims of war.
>   *We need to live in defence of people and creation.*

For I believe in the interwovenness of life:
>   Creator and creatures . . . Breath and prayer
>   Cosmic and individual . . . Food and freedom
>   West, North, East, South . . .
>   Sexuality and spirituality . . . ecology and theology.

I therefore commit myself,
together with other concerned people everywhere,
to take care of Mother Earth.
To advocate for peace and justice.
To choose and celebrate Life!

These things I believe. Amen.

ELIZABETH S. TAPIA
ASIA

The Grain is Ripe

The grain is ripe:
the harvest comes!
good seed of hope,
your time is now
justice will stream
from hill and river,
more than you dream
and running over!

The righteous God
gives this and more:
grace is the mode,
mercy the key,
God comes in truth,
the sharpest laser
to scan the earth,
to take our measure.

The work of peace
is all for all,
face turned to face,

in open trust,
all famine gone
and thirst and bleeding –
the harvest comes
from love's good seeding.

SHIRLEY ERENA MURRAY
AOTEAROA NEW ZEALAND

Ever fashioning,
ever renewing God;
may we never lose
our sense of awe,
wonder and sheer amazement
at this universe
of which we are
so insignificant a part.
Yet we may never be so overawed
that we forget
that great as you are,
and vast and intricate
as are your works,
you know and love
each one of us,
and we are ever in your care.

EDMUND BANYARD
ENGLAND

Not ours, O Lord, but yours;
The earth belongs to you.

We mine the copper, gold and iron,
We take the minerals from the earth,
Coal, wood, and water; soil and clay.
We use these gifts from day to day
But
Not ours, O Lord, they're yours;
The earth belongs to you.

From orchard trees and soft brown earth,
From bush and cane, from branch and stalk,
From rivers, seas and grinding mill
We take all good things as we will
But
Not ours, O Lord, they're yours;
The earth belongs to you.

We marvel at the swelling seas,
We gaze into the night-time sky,
By painter's brush or poet's tongue
We think they all to us belong
But
Not ours, O Lord, they're yours;
The earth belongs to you.

DONALD HILTON
ENGLAND

The season of growth

Not Spring,
when tender shoots
are quickly trampled down
and unsuspected frosts destroy;
when bursting life spawns myriads
to keep the few
and thus begets the tragedy of death
within the hope of birth.

Nor Summer months,
when all creation sates itself:
languid, replete and over-satisfied;
long hours when warmth invites unseemly ease
or, sun-denied, breed disappointment.

Not Autumn,
when ripened fruitfulness
reveals the hint of quick decay,
and sombre beauty of the leaves
(so long romanticised in poetry and song)
speaks out for death and death's decay.
The Autumn beauty of the trees
invites a requiem and not a feast.

No, Winter is the season of our growth:
creation held in quiet suspense,
pausing for fresh breath
and new endeavour;
when bulbs build up resources for their life
and searching roots reserve their strength,
looking to the rhythm of another year;
when stem and flower fall broken to the ground
and seeming loss is richer gain
as earth receives its food
to rise again next year.

Winter is neither death
nor even slumber.
Winter is the season of our growth.

DONALD HILTON
ENGLAND

New Responsibility

Great Spirit,
still brooding over the world –

We hear the cry of the earth,
we see the sorrow of land
raped and plundered in our greed
for its varied resources.

We hear the cry of the waters,
we see the sorrow of stream and ocean
polluted by the poisons
we release into them.

We hear the cry of the animals,
we see the sorrow of bird, fish and beast
needlessly suffering and dying
to serve our profit or sport or vanity.

Please teach us

a proper sensitivity
towards your feeling creation

a proper simplicity
in the way we live in our environment

a proper appreciation
of the connectedness of all things

a proper respect
for the shalom of the universe.

We turn from our arrogant ways
to seek you again, Creator of all life.
Redeem us – and redeem your world
and heal its wounds and dry its tears.
May our response to you bear fruit
in a fresh sense of responsibility
towards everything you have created.

KATE COMPSTON
ENGLAND

A God for all Seasons

Springtime God, coming alive within us, like pale shoots
                thrusting through frozen earth,
    we need your persistent love
    to disturb the impacted soil of our hearts' rigidity.

Summer God, growing luxuriously, blossoming with heady
    scents,
            holding us in your warm embrace,
    we need these times of perceived presence
    to draw upon in cooler seasons.

Autumn God, falling and dying in Christ,
            etched with the colours of vulnerability,
    we need the fellowship of your wounds
    to dignify our brokenness.

Winter God, dormant and distant,
            starkly challenging our self-absorption,
    we need your austerity
    to nudge us into a warm compassion for your suffering
        ones.

KATE COMPSTON
ENGLAND

Creation Covenant

Voice 1:   The Universe in its awesomeness, reflects the loving, dreaming and shaping of the Divine Artist, who looks upon what has been created, sees how good it is and celebrates its life.

Voice 2:   Scripture affirms the value of human beings, within nature's intertwining tapestry, for we who are formed in the cosmic dust, have the breath of God within us.

Voice 3:   Each one of us is Adam and Eve responsible for nurturing the life and resources of this greening planet.

Voice 4:   Each of us like the woman, and her husband Noah, is entrusted with the survival of the species.

Voice 5:   Each of us is called by God to nurture and protect Asia's and [name your own country] sacred soil, water, air, living things for generations yet unborn.

All: **We commit ourselves**
To join with you, O God
To nurture
The plants and animals,
The elements,
The sacred womb of sea and soil.
We offer you our ability to create and
Our potential to release
people's loving energies
For the benefit of all creation.
We sing with you the song of the universe!
We dance with you the dance of life!
We are yours,
And you in us are hope
For the renewing of nature
Through the healing of the nations

FROM *WORSHIP RESOURCES FOR ASIA SUNDAY, 1993*

In the garden, on the farms

In the garden, on the farms
Signs of life are showing;
Lambs and buds, the calves and trees
Praise the God of growing.

Kowhais gild the native bush,
Alpine meadows blossom,
Ferns unfold and mosses fruit –
Signs of God's great kingdom.

At our country's time of spring
May we see our duty
To protect the heritage
Of our forest's beauty.

Help us care much more, O Lord,
For the unprotected,
For the young, the old, the poor –
All who are neglected.

Then God's fragile plant will bloom
In our selfish nation;
People will respect the weak –
Honour God's creation.

BILL WALLACE
AOTEAROA NEW ZEALAND

A Liturgy for Harvest Thanksgiving

The gifts are brought to the table or altar and are lifted up as they are referred to.

To you, Creator, God, we bring *earth*
symbol of this sacred land of Aotearoa pledged by Treaty
to be shared with justice.

To you parenting God, we bring *water*
remembering the precious gift of seas, lakes and rivers.

To you God of warming love and searing truth we bring *fire*
to remind us of the honouring and betrayal of each other and
    of you.

To you God of life and creativity we offer *air*,
breath of our lungs, inspiration of our spirits,
symbol of religious and political freedom.

To you God of growth we bring these *seeds*
signs of the enormous potential within human beings,
hope of its flowering and fruiting in the lives of the people.

To you God of covenant we offer the *Treaty of Waitangi*,
cornerstone of the nation, guide for the bicultural journey.

All: We are yours O God, enable us as responsible, loved,
        loving and creative people, to create a just, empowering
        and celebrating society in Aotearoa. Amen.

PACK ONE OF THE *WORSHIP RESOURCES*
AOTEAROA NEW ZEALAND

Dearest Earth, Our Mother

Dearest Earth, our Mother,
      Kind and bountiful;
      Loving all your children,
      Giving life to all.
      We are all your *whanau*
      Joined by spiral thread,
      Binding all the living,
      Linking all the dead.

Earth will live forever
      Ancient wisdom said;
      Modern wisdom tells us
      Earth may soon be dead.
      Mother Earth lies bleeding
      Tortured by our hands,
      Seeking endless profits
      From the finite land.

A–o–te–a–ro–a,
      Sacred island space;
      Home where God in nature
      Shows a furrowed face;
      Land for all our children
      Born and yet to be –
      May your weeping help us
      Long to set you free!

BILL WALLACE
AOTEAROA NEW ZEALAND

Come to this Christmas singing!

Come to this Christmas singing!
Come to a birthday, bringing
gifts from our country's treasure,
beauty of shell and stone:
> wisdom the old have taught us,
> laughter the young have brought us,
> love to surround a manger,
> making this Child our own.

Wealth of our land and water,
riches of race and culture –
these be our gold and incense
offered for Christmas Day:
> where we make peace, declare it,
> where we have much, to share it,
> *aroha* warm our hearts, and
> *aroha* be our way.

Here where the sheep are grazing,
where summer sun is blazing
harvests for others ripen –
food for the world can grow:
> Christ of a cold December,
> quicken us to remember
> poverty in a stable,
> need, like the sting of snow.

(Tune: 'Workers' Carol'.)

SHIRLEY ERENA MURRAY
AOTEAROA NEW ZEALAND

Brother Sun

Brother Sun shining on the golden fields of harvest time
Baking the crops under his sharp rays
Brightening the sky from horizon to horizon

Sister Moon lets out a midnight eeriness
Dappling everything in a silver moonlight
The tranquillity is extreme

Brother Wind and Brother Air hurrying the auburn leaves
Occasionally they will sweep them up into the sky twisting
      round and round
Until dropping them back leaving them spinning in their own
      light

Sister Water all purity no deception
So clear clean and beautiful
So helpful, always merry, always moving
Foams up when shaken but then dissolves into an array of
      minerals

Brother Fire's red hot flames warm people's houses on cold
      nights
Burns unwanted crops and weeds
Spreading their ashes on the grass
Letting you know of his power

Sister Earth
Full of wonderful curiosities
Bright colours and fantastical mysteries
All plants and creatures belong to her
And displays all her belongings under a canopy of life.

CATHERINE BALL, AGED 12
ENGLAND

An Earth Charter for the Churches of Aotearoa New Zealand

Preamble: This Charter is from a *Pakeha* (white New Zealander) perspective. *Pakeha* are *tangata Tiriti*, or signing partners to the Treaty of Waitangi 1840. This solemn covenant between the indigenous people, *tangata wenua* or *Maori*, and the British Crown, obligates the Pakeha to ensure that Maori have control over all things Maori, including their language, land, forests, fisheries and other natural and cultural treasures. This is the principle of *te tino rangatiratanga*. In the light of this commitment and in profound respect for indigenous spirituality and understanding of creation, we offer this Charter as a contribution to the Christian responsibility to care for creation.

We believe that God has created and continually sustains the Earth.

We are Pakeha New Zealanders, who stand under the authority and spirit of the Treaty of Waitangi.

We declare ourselves open to find new ways to sustain the life of this planet, and especially of Aotearoa New Zealand; to be co-workers with God to maintain the life, health, and dignity of each human person, in harmony with life, health, and dignity of the natural world.

We confess that human ignorance, greed, and exploitation degrade and endanger the Earth.

We confess that the whole Earth suffers from the violence of war, greedy business practices and carelessness in a cycle of pain, injustice, poverty, deprivation, and death. 'All of creation groans with pain.'

We seek to build a wholesome environment in Aotearoa and beyond our shores where all creation may flourish, enhanced by peace and justice, the beauty and diversity of life in the world cherished, giving healing and honour to the Earth.

We seek solidarity and partnership with peoples of all faiths and ideologies who are engaged in the care and liberation of the Earth.

We will translate our words into programmes of action, and commit ourselves to a lifestyle which the Earth can sustain.

We commit ourselves to join, through the Spirit, the reconciling work which the One Living God is now doing in all the world, a rule of love, peace and justice proclaimed and lived by Jesus Christ, and embodied in and through the community of faith which follows Him.

FROM THE JUSTICE, PEACE AND THE INTEGRITY
OF CREATION WORKING GROUP
OF THE NEW ZEALAND COUNCIL FOR MISSION AND
ECUMENICAL CO-OPERATION

Earth Prayer

I am your mother: do not neglect me!
Children, protect me – I need your trust;
     my breath is your breath,
     my death is your death,
ashes to ashes, dust into dust.

I am your nurture: do not destroy me!
Love and enjoy me, savour my fruit;
     my good is your good,
     my food is your food,
water and flower, branches and root.

I am your lodging: do not abuse me!
Tenderly use me, soothing my scars;
     my health is your health,
     my wealth is your wealth,
shining with promise, set among stars.

God is our maker: do not deny God,
challenge, defy God, threaten this place:
life is to cherish –
care, or we perish!
I am your mother, tears on my face . . .

SHIRLEY ERENA MURRAY
AOTEAROA NEW ZEALAND

Lord Speak to Us

Lord speak to us
through the beauty of the earth:
from the rising of the sun
till dusk
and the moon and the stars
at night,
your beauty is there
for all to see.

Open our eyes Lord,
to drink in the wonders
so that we may reflect
your beauty
in kindness
and humility
and show the world
your patience and gentleness
by our actions.

PATRICIA PREECE
ENGLAND

We believe that God has given human beings dignity, talents and a homeland, so that they may share in God's creation, and have responsibility with Him for taking care of the world. Therefore, they have social, political and economic systems, arts and sciences, and a spirit which seeks after the true God. But human beings have sinned, and they misuse these gifts, destroying the relationship between themselves, all creatures, and God. Therefore, they must depend on the saving grace of Jesus Christ. He will deliver humankind from sin, will set the oppressed free and make them equal, that all may become new creatures in Christ, and the world His Kingdom, full of justice, peace and joy.

PRESBYTERIAN CHURCH IN TAIWAN

In Our Land

In our land,
Poppies do not spring
From atoms of young blood,
So gaudily where men have died:
In our land
Stiletto cane blades
Sink into our hearts
And drink our blood.

On our land,
Sin is not deep,
And bends before the truth,
Asking repentantly for pardon:
In our land,
The ugly stain
That blotted Eden garden
Is sunk deep only.

In our land
Storms do not strike
For territory's fences,
Elbow room, nor breathing spaces:
In our land
The hurricane
Of clashes break our ranks
For tint of eye.

In our land
We do not breed
That taloned king, the eagle,
Nor make emblazonry of lions;
In our land,
The black birds
And the chickens of our mountains
Speak our dreams.

HAROLD TELEMAQUE

Remembrance

In remembrance of those –
throughout time, all over the world –
who have died in war,
    we pray urgently today
    that children, women and men
    may become makers of peace.

We pray for children growing up
in violent surroundings
or thinking, talking and playing in warlike ways.
    God, give to your people a new challenge,
    new ways in which to test their strength –
    in sharing power and risking non-violence.

We pray for women who are silent
while their male partners engage
in any part of the business of war.

God, give to your people a new courage
to question accepted dogma,
and dream about the things that make for peace.

We pray for men brought up to believe
that might is manly – and for men who think otherwise
and so are labelled cowardly or weak.
God, give to your people a new determination
to struggle for justice and peace
instead of for 'extra shares' and superiority.

O God, we pray for –
new awareness of the battlefield within us
new ways of challenging aggressive instincts
new thought-patterns, language and ideas
new appreciation of the world as one community
new methods of dialogue and negotiation
new attempts to befriend those different from
ourselves
new readiness to forgive and reconcile,
new visions, new love, new hope . . .
and a new faith that the peace that passes understanding
can reach out from within us to embrace the world.

KATE COMPSTON
ENGLAND

Hiroshima

To remember the past is to commit oneself to the future. To remember Hiroshima is to abhor nuclear war. To remember Hiroshima is to commit oneself to peace. Let us promise our fellow human beings that we will work untiringly for disarmament and the banishing of all nuclear weapons; let us replace violence and hate with confidence and caring. Peace must always be the aim; peace pursued and protected in all circumstances. Let us embark upon the steep and difficult path of peace.

POPE JOHN PAUL II

Cease Fire

Like many a parent
  He waits – longing – hopeful.
Over the world hangs a strange silence
  Guns are laid down
  Boats slumber in the harbour
  Planes rest their engines in the hangars.
Still He waits – longing – hopeful
  for His children's return.

It is quiet – a cease fire
  but underneath the hush
  lies unrest – a turmoil
  of the pain and anger,
  the unshed tears
  of grief and bitterness.
All around is destruction
  mutilated bodies and shattered buildings
  the stench of death and fear.

Like many a parent
  He cries at the futility
  of it all.
He yearns to enfold the world in His arms

to share its sorrow
to heal its wounds
but still He waits
for their return.

Like many a parent
He understands the loss
and knows the high price of victory.
True liberation and peace
already cost Him a Son.
He waits – longing – hopeful
to comfort and console
to offer His bread not guns
forgiveness not anger
love not hatred
joy not pain
laughter not tears
freedom not captivity.

Unlike any parent
He offers peace,
not just the absence of war –
silence – a mere cease fire
but His eternal Shalom
for His children
when they return.

CARYS HUMPHREYS
WALES AND TAIWAN

Peace

Peace is in the heart of God
but how shall we find peace between people?
There can be no flower of peace
from the seeds of discord;
there can be no fruit of peace
from the root of injustice;
there can be no reaping of peace
from the sowing of oppression.
But when in our thoughts
we honour God and our neighbours,
when in our words
we encourage those who are lonely or depressed,
when in our actions
we seek justice and freedom for all,
then peace breaks out with happiness
in all the places where people meet
and women and men, young and old,
join in the tongues of all the nations
to praise the Prince of Peace,
Jesus, Emmanuel, God alongside us.

JOHN JOHANSEN-BERG
ENGLAND

O God our Father

God our Father,
save our shores from the weapons of death
our lands from what may deny our young ones love and
        freedom.
Let the seas of the Pacific Ocean
carry messages of peace and goodwill.
Turn away from our midst any unkind and brutal practices.
Let our children swim, and breathe the fresh air
that is filled by the Holy Spirit.

O Lord Jesus
bless all who are makers of that inner peace
which breaks down the barriers of hatred;
and unite us with the open arms of your cross,
that all the peoples of the world may live happily together.
Amen.

SIONE AMANAKI HAVEA
TONGA

Reconciliation

Across the barriers that divide race from race:
        Reconcile us, O Christ, by your cross.
Across the barriers that divide the rich from the poor:
        Reconcile us, O Christ, by your cross.
Across the barriers that divide people of different faiths:
        Reconcile us, O Christ, by your cross.
Across the barriers that divide Christians:
        Reconcile us, O Christ, by your cross.
Across the barriers that divide men and women, young and old:
        Reconcile us, O Christ, by your cross.

Confront us, O Christ, with the hidden prejudices and fears
which deny and betray our prayers. Enable us to see the causes
of strife. Remove from us all false sense of superiority. Teach
us to grow in unity with all God's children. Amen.

VANCOUVER ASSEMBLY WORSHIP BOOK, WCC, 1983

Peacemakers?

What was it like, Jesus
when others
wanted peace at all costs
without knowing the cost of real Peace

when they expected you
to condemn
the woman who sprawled,
shrinking, at your feet
with the cry 'Adulterer!'
ringing in her ears
bracing herself for the first stone
to slam into her body?

What was it like to know you could buy peace
by following the rules
faithfully but blindly,
as the accusing, watchful eyes
demanded?

What was it like
to take the risk
of restoring Peace in the house of prayer
arousing the anger of vested interests
disturbing the comfortable
profit-making ventures of the powerful?

What was it like to refuse to satisfy
the militant agenda of the
zealots among your own disciples
to ride in humble dignity
upon an ass
knowing only some would understand
the implications?

What was it like, Jesus
to watch us trading justice for peace
and trading Peace for gain
condemning the weak
whose sin is no worse than our own
while allowing the powerful
to rob and oppress the poor?

You were strong enough
to fight for justice
and not to fight for power.

What would it be like, Jesus
if we were to be open to your strength

and so could be peacemakers
unafraid to shatter
the peacefulness
of injustice?

SUSAN JONES
AOTEAROA NEW ZEALAND

Prayer for Peace

We ask you to lead us in the way of peace, dear Lord,
but then in so many ways we choose the way of war.

There is a war in thoughts
when we are in inner turmoil or think ill of others;
there is a war of words
whenever our sharp tongues hurt;
there is a war in actions
when tribalism, nationalism, pride and greed
turn our neighbours into enemies.
Forgive us, Lord.

Lead us in the way of true peace
as we seek to understand our neighbours, near and far;
as we work for justice in the community,
local and international;
as we seek the peace that cares and encourages
and that conserves the beauty and fruitfulness
of our common homeland, mother earth.

JOHN JOHANSEN-BERG
ENGLAND

Affirmation of peace and justice

All: I believe in God, who is love and who has given the earth to all people.

I believe in Jesus Christ, who came to heal us, and to free us from all forms of oppression.

I believe in the Spirit of God, who works in and through all who are turned towards the truth.

I believe in the community of faith, which is called to be at the service of all people.

I believe in God's promise to finally destroy the power of sin in us all, and to establish the kingdom of justice and peace for all mankind.

Group A: I do not believe in the right of the strongest, nor the force of arms, nor the power of oppression.

Group B: I believe in human rights, in the solidarity of all people, in the power of non-violence.

Group A: I do not believe in racism, in the power that comes from wealth and privilege, or in any established order that enslaves.

Group B: I believe that all men and women are equally human, that order based on violence and injustice is not order.

Group A:	I do not believe that war and hunger are inevitable and peace unattainable.
Group B:	I believe in beauty of simplicity, in love with open hands, in peace on earth.
All:	I do not believe that suffering needs to be in vain, that death is the end, that the disfigurement of the world is what God intended. But I dare to believe, always and in spite of everything, in God's power to transform and transfigure, fulfilling the promise of a new heaven and a new earth where justice and peace will flourish.

ADAPTED FROM A CREED FROM INDONESIA

To look at anything
If you would know that thing,
You must look at it long:
To look at this green and say
'I have seen spring in these
woods,' will not do – you must
be the thing you see:
You must be the dark snakes of
stems and ferny plumes of leaves.
You must enter in
to the small silences between
the leaves.
You must take your time
and touch the very peace
they issue from

JOHN MOFFITT

Peace Child

Peace Child,
in the sleep of the night
in the dark before light
you come,
in the silence of the stars
in the violence of wars –
Saviour, your name

Peace Child,
to the road and the storm
to the gun and the bomb
you come,
through the hate and the hurt,
through the hunger and dirt –
bearing a dream

Peace Child,
to our dark and our sleep
to the conflict we reap
now come –
be your dream born alive,
held in hope, wrapped in love:
God's true shalom.

SHIRLEY ERENA MURRAY
AOTEAROA NEW ZEALAND

A Child

a child
appeared in my dreams
with Kamunggay* in her hands
she was going to heal the wounds
of those hurt
by life's deprivation
      alienation
      dehumanization

a child
surfaced in my hopes
with a sweet smile on her face
she was going to spread sunshine
on those imprisoned
by life's agony
      anxiety
      brutality

a child
stood at the horizon of my tomorrows
with the sun, the moon and the stars
in her eyes
she was going to deliver fire
to those challenged
by life's struggles
      cycles
      miracles

today the child
of my dreams, hopes, tomorrows
is born
God remains pleased
with the world
long live the child

*A healing herb.

CARLOS GASPAR

Let Justice Flow

'Let justice flow . . .' (Amos 5:24)

We live in a world where four fifths of the population do not have enough and the other one fifth have all the power; where the global institutions control trade, banking, development programmes and aid based on Western economic theory rather than human need; where the poorest countries pay more in debt repayments than they receive in aid; where the rich slide comfortably into spiritual and moral decline. And we wonder where God is.

Poverty, Pain and the Option for the Poor, the titles of Part Two's subsections, spring off the pages of writers on these global issues.

Poverty can give clarity to spiritual thought. Understanding the Holy Spirit is easy for the garbage worker. A parable Jesus used about sowing seeds makes sense to an agricultural community. Prison and hunger help Ed de la Torre ('To Hunger and Thirst for Justice') to describe his desire for justice.

Contributions from people experiencing wealth are more searching, questioning and confused. Spirituality is perhaps suppressed by guilt: 'Lord forgive' ('My Prayer'), 'We are sorry' ('For between us and you a great chasm has been fixed'), 'What step are you gonna take to try and set things right?' ('Stolen Land').

The pain of both these experiences is expressed here. The greater pain is that of the poor, as expressed by Fan Yew Teng

('Sing to us Mama'), yet the pain of the wealthy also cries out to God: 'Teach us to be fully human, open to each other's needs' ('God of Freedom').

The Option for the Poor suggests a meeting point. "To be a Christian one has to take sides' ('The Option for the Poor'); one has to understand that 'the Gospel has the power to set people free, that the Good News to the poor is a message of liberation' ('Communities of Freedom'). Liberation for us all!

Not to take this option for the poor is to opt out: 'It is cold – Get more cardboard friend', as expressed by Hazel Down ('It is cold'). Sitting on the fence is not a Kingdom position, although we may be called to 'watch and pray'.

Let these stories, thoughts and prayers help you into the world of the victims. You may become aware that you also are a victim, and in that you may find solidarity. In solidarity we can pray.

MARTIN GAGE

POVERTY

A Parable

In one of the study sessions of the BCC (Base Christian Community) in a popular neighbourhood of a big city, the counsellor, speaking of the Holy Spirit, asked: 'How do you understand the action of the Spirit? How do you explain it?'

A poor working man, whose job was to gather and burn the garbage of the city, raised his hand.

'I understand it like this: in my job I have continually to gather the garbage, pile it up and destroy it. I have been doing this for years and I try to keep the fire burning continually; nevertheless, there are times when it seems that the fire has gone out completely, but I know that, underneath, a few embers continue to burn. Regardless of how large the garbage deposit is, the fire is never completely extinguished. I think that humanity is like the garbage and that the Holy Spirit is like the fire. The Church must always act as I do in my work: it must gather together humanity and put it in contact with the Spirit, so as to purify it until it is no longer garbage.

'The Church should never lose hope, even when the fire cannot be seen and the garbage is plentiful. She must be convinced that the fire continues to burn below – that it will never go out.'

JOSÉ MARINS

Central American Lord's Prayer

Our Father
who is in us here on earth
holy is your name
in the hungry who share their bread and their song.
Your kingdom come,
a generous land where confidence and truth reign.
Let us do your will
being a cool breeze for those who sweat.
You are giving us our daily bread
when we manage to get back our lands
or to get a fairer wage.
Forgive us
for keeping silent in the face of injustice
and for burying our dreams.
Don't let us fall into the temptation
of taking up the same arms as the enemy,
but deliver us from evil which disunites us.
And we shall have believed in humanity and in life
and we shall have known your kingdom
which is being built for ever and ever.

CENTRAL AMERICAN LORD'S PRAYER (SHORTENED)

My Prayer

O God,

you have sown the seeds of love in my heart
but I have not watered it with my tears –
Lord forgive.

You have shown me hungry children
and I have fed only my friends –
Lord forgive.

You have shown me the homeless
and I have cared only for my own home –
Lord forgive.

You have shown me the naked
but I have only clothed myself –
Lord forgive.

You have shown me the wounded
and I have been only concerned with my own pain –
Lord forgive.

You have shown me the friendless
and I have nurtured my own friendships –
Lord forgive,

You have shown me the bereaved
and I have sought out others to comfort me –
Lord forgive.

You have shown me those who do not know your love
and I have failed to share that which you have given me –
Lord forgive and help me to obey.

ETHEL JENKINS
ENGLAND

Stolen Land

From Tierra del Fuego to Ungava Bay
the history of betrayal continues to today
the spirit of Almighty Voice, the ghost of Anna Mae
call like thunder from the mountains – you can hear
them say
It's a stolen land

Apartheid in Arizona, slaughter in Brazil
if bullets don't get good PR there's other ways to kill
kidnap all the children, put 'em in a foreign system
bring them up in no-man's land where no one really
wants them
It's a stolen land

stolen land – but it's all we've got
stolen land – and there's no going back
stolen land – and we'll never forget
stolen land – and we're not through yet

In my mind I catch a picture – big black raven in the sky
looking at the ocean – sail reflected in black eye –
sail as white as heroin, white like weathered bones –
rum and guns and smallpox gonna change the face
of home
In this stolen land . . .

If you're like me you'd like to think we've learned
from our mistakes
enough to know we can't play god with others' lives
at stake
so now we've all discovered the world wasn't only
made for whites
what step are you gonna take to try and set things
right
In this stolen land

stolen land – but it's all we've got
stolen land – and there's no going back
stolen land – and we'll never forget
stolen land – and we're not through yet

BRUCE COCKBURN

Prescription for Development

Our National General Assembly
was in deep mortification.
An insensitive journalist
(from some northern region)
had branded our country
a model of Underdevelopment.

How to gain recognition
as a developed nation
pondered our President.
The answer? – Commission
a group of technocrats
to study, possibly remedy
this intolerable situation.

What you have here, sir
are too many green hills –
a surfeit of lush vegetation.
Trees are fine but unproductive
and hills are an impediment.

There are too many canefields
and too many plantations.
We do not know what development
is, but an agricultural economy
is the badge of underdevelopment.

Your beaches are beautiful, sir
but lack proper utilisation;
there are no tourists, hotels
or any high rise apartments.

Your streets are all traffic-free
and your towns too quiet;
your people seem stress-free
and a trifle too contented.

They eat fruits and vegetables
and drink natural water
which we are shocked to discover
is indecently clean and pure.

So what we recommend sir –
for your race to develop –
is first massive deforestation
followed by massive importation.

You need juggernauts, bull-
dozers and belching factories
condos and fast-food chains
and hordes of snooping tourists.

You must import mineral water
and a medium sized nuclear reactor,
and a score of foreign psychiatrists
to service your expat industrialists.

We beg your pardon, but pollution
is the hallmark of development.
To qualify as an advanced country
you have to boast a proper degree
of noise/smog/dumps and derangement.

With no hesitation, our President
embraced their recommendation.
In ear-muffs he now sits
in a haze-shrouded apartment.

High above, but not quite beyond
the city's teeming shout and bustle;
with a glass of Perrier water
he pops tranquillisers by the bottle.

He has a direct open line
to his Swiss psychiatrist;
he keeps an emergency canister
of oxygen taped to his wrist.

By grinning from ear to ear
as he chomps on his hamburger
Mr President is now all glee.
For that damned foreign journalist
has just declared our country:
'The Developing Nation of the Year'.

CECIL RAJENDRA
MALAYSIA

To Hunger and Thirst for Justice

I have never been this hungry before
pain burning my guts, searing my back

Food is doubly delicious
tuyo or crispy pata
corn soup and sinigang
turo-turo meals and banquets

To starve after justice
To ache for it, like food, frantic for life itself

How long can men live without eating
two weeks or more, they say.
But would such be living?
Too weak to rise from sleep
to read Bible and newspaper
to write with real meaning and beauty
to share and master the earth
to sing in the sun?

How long can men live without justice?
Can we ask them to wait again
while we ponderously weigh issues
which are complex, we say, and take time
which cannot be rushed
because we fear to be one-sided
etcetera?

Blessed are those who hunger and thirst after justice
for they shall be satisfied.

But when, O Lord, and how?

ED DE LA TORRE
PHILIPPINES

Project Report: A dramatic poem

(A missionary working in Lagos, Nigeria, received a grant
to provide Christmas cheer for old people. He helped to
share the gifts and received an unexpected blessing. He is
recording on tape a report explaining how the grant was
spent.)

Speaker: 'To Projects Officer, PO Box, etc. etc.:

'Dear Sir,

'The grant you gave was used as follows: We
purchased thirty plastic bags. In each we placed a pound
of rice, some tea, dried beans, St Matthew's gospel in the
local language, sugar and salt, a box of matches, tinned
tomato puree, local leaves resembling spinach, bananas,
oranges, some palm oil, and a greeting card.

'The funds, we trust, were wisely spent; the list of aged-
people checked and double-checked in case of fraud. The
bags were packed on Christmas Eve, and taken round by
volunteers on Christmas Day. Each team included one at
least who spoke the local language. I myself took part . . .'

(The speaker stops dictating and starts remembering.)

Old woman, please forgive.
We came to help. I never knew your home
Was bare, so very bare; the walls unpainted
Concrete: never thought we'd scare you stiff,
We strangers bearing gifts. You saw and dreaded
My whitish face and khaki shorts, my thin
Thin lips and pointed nose. Was it police?
Or taxmen? Trouble – yes, official trouble!
We gave you such a fright on Christmas morning
Attempting to deliver one of thirty
Plastic bags containing . . . never mind . . .
For once you understood, you offered thanks
In long melodious words and solemn gestures
Centuries old. You greeted Khaki shorts
(Who hardly knows the local language) kindly,
Maternally, a queen beside your charcoal
Fire: then you smiled and made your farewell curtsey
Slowly and gently, being old, but smoothly,
As though the years had spared your maidenhood.
You blessed me then. We went our way unsnubbed
And you unpatronized.

Let's try again.

(And so back to the dictation.)

'To Projects Officer, PO Box, etc. etc.:

'Dear Sir,
    'The grant you gave was used as follows . . .'

JOHN COUTTS
NIGERIA

The Bible and Economics – A Dialogue for Today

Don't seize control.

A. When you make your neighbour a loan of any sort, you shall not go into his house to fetch his pledge. You shall stand outside, and the man to whom you made the loan shall bring the pledge out to you (Deuteronomy 24:10).

B. When you make a loan of any sort to a poor country, you shall not send in a team of experts to reorganise the economy. The people who live there shall bring proposals for change.

There is a limit.

A. If ever you take your neighbour's garment in pledge, you shall restore it to him before the sun goes down; for that is his only covering, it is his mantle for his body; in what else shall he sleep? (Exodus 22:26).

B. If ever you are taking interest repayments from your neighbours, you shall restore them their dignity. There is a limit: you may not strip the poor naked.

The means of survival.

A. No one shall take a mill or an upper millstone in pledge; for he would be taking a life on pledge (Deuteronomy 24:6).

B. No one shall take the land which used to grow corn for poor people to eat bread, and grow flowers for export instead – it is like taking people's lives in pledge.

Protection for the poorest.

A. When you reap your harvest in your field, and have forgotten a sheaf, you shall not go back to get it; it shall be for the sojourner, and the fatherless and the widow (Deuteronomy 24:19).

B. When you are trying to balance your economy, and you have left subsidies on basic foodstuffs, you shall not go back and remove them. They shall be for those who cannot survive without them.

Employment.

A. You shall not oppress a hired servant who is poor and needy. You shall give him his hire on the day he earns it, before the sun goes down (for he is poor, and sets his heart upon it) (Deuteronomy 24:14).

B. You shall not deny a living wage to those who have only their labour to survive on. They have set their heart on it and need it today, and not in five years' time.

Double standards.

A. You shall not have in your bag two kinds of weight, a large and a small. A full and just weight you shall have, a full and just measure (Deuteronomy 25:13).

B. You shall not have in your economic theory two kinds of standard, one for the rich and the other for the poor. You shall not make poor people devalue their currency, their labour and their lives while you protect your own.

Listen to the poor.

A. If the poor person cries to me, I will hear, for I am compassionate (Exodus 22:27).

B. If the poor person cries to you, you shall hear, and be compassionate.

JANET MORLEY
ENGLAND

Dust, Goats and Grandfather Clocks

Dust, goats and grandfather clocks;
mark the former government policy
of separate development
in comfortable sounding
homelands.
In reality, these were
dustbowls of poverty
and open sewers of disease.
Overgrazed land
where families couldn't even subsist
without sent home wages
from migrant labourers.
On the day of the revolution,
the strings of puppet government
finally cut,
the status symbols of oppression
fell into the people's hands
and grandfather clocks
into the backs of trucks.

Liberating Spirit,
who whipped up the winds of change,
hover over the land
as new rain falls,
so that maize is raised up from dust,
and oversee the ripening
of the promised harvest
of freedom.

JANET LEES
ENGLAND AND SOUTH AFRICA

The Parable of the Sower

In 1966 a Nicaraguan priest, Ernesto Cardinal, with a Colombian poet, William Agudeb, and his wife, Teresita, began a small Christian commune in Solentiname. Local campesinos began to come to their church. Instead of a homily on the Gospel reading, there was a discussion.

Matthew 13:1–13.

Ernesto: 'You are campesinos and you will be able to understand very well this parable of the seed.'

Don Jose: 'The seed is a living thing. You don't sow dead seeds. And so, as I see it, the message is a living thing.'

Oscar: 'The seed is also something to eat. People sow grains that feed us. The words of Jesus are grains that he scatters in the wind, to feed us all.'

Donald: 'The seed is a tiny, wrinkled, ugly thing, and anyone who doesn't know better might think that it's useless. And it's the same with the word of God, it seems to me, when the person that receives it doesn't know what it contains.'

William (with his son Juan in his arms): 'And there's another special thing about the seed, as I see it. It's not only a living thing but it's the transmission of life.'

Natalia, the midwife: 'We are all seeds. Seeds who produce more seeds.'

Oscar: 'Christ rose from the dead because he was a healthy seed. In the harvest we have seen that not every seed is born but only the good seeds, the nice healthy ones. And so, if we're going to rise from the dead like Christ we must be the same kind of seed that he was.'

Olivia: 'I think that Jesus spoke of the seed because he was talking to us campesinos. If he had been talking for the rich he would have used examples that they would have understood very well. But he used this example of the seed because he was talking our language. He was talking about seeds and birds that eat the grains and plants that die of oversoaking and of swamps, because that's our language.'

Old Tomas: 'And when we hear the message and we forget it, it's like the corn that the birds ate. You sow now, and tomorrow when you go to look there's nothing at all. The birds ate it all. The birds are the devil that carried off the message that had been sown.'

Marcelino: 'These words about the seed that we are hearing here are the same seeds, and maybe we hadn't realized it. If we hear these words the seed of the kingdom is buried in us, he says. But he speaks of the kingdom only for those who have ears.'

Julio: 'I see one thing. The seed alone, without the land, doesn't do anything. So this doctrine without us is of no use. Without us there is no kingdom of heaven.'

NICARAGUA
EDITED BY PHILIP AND SALLY SCHARPER

'For between us and you a great chasm has been fixed' (Luke 16:26)

Between us and them,
between us and the million
named Lazarus,
a great chasm has been fixed:
and we would almost thank you,
almost thank you for our security,
our stout walls,
that we can wind our car windows up
when we're away from home . . .
. . . except for the ache
inside us.
For between us and you, Jesus,
lies that same chasm,
and we are sorry.
We shut the window, Spirit,
against you,
and we are sorry.
We would rather believe, Creator,
that you made Grasmere,
but not Bermondsey,
and we are sorry.
Forgive us God.
We thank you
that the hand reaching across the chasm
is yours.

BOB WARWICKER
ENGLAND

PAIN

Sing to us, Mama . . .

Mama, where are these killer birds from?

From far away, my love.

Mama, why do they come so many times?

They want to kill all of us, perhaps.

Why Mama?

I don't know, love; they are at war with us.

But they've killed Grandpa and Grandma and my friends, and the cats, the flowers and the trees . . . they've done nothing wrong . . .

I know, my love, they were killed, but not because they've done anything wrong . . .

Then, why, why, why, Mama?

Simply because they were here.

Mama, I am sick, hungry and thirsty . . .

Yes, love, I know. We are all sick, hungry and thirsty. They have destroyed our water, our food, our baby milk powder, our hospitals and clinics, our doctors and nurses . . .

They have also destroyed my school, Mama.

Yes, love, and our mosque, our house, and Tony's church . . . their thunder and lightning have covered up the sun with smoke, noise and blood . . . and fire and fury . . .

Can't we go away from this heap of bricks, Mama?

No, love, the roads are blocked by debris and rubble, and they have destroyed the buses, taxis and lorries.

Mama, where is Papa?

He has gone to fight the killer birds.

Will he come back to us soon, Mama?

I don't know. I hope so. Be a brave girl.

I miss Papa, Mama.

Yes, I know, for I miss him too. Now, be a good girl, give some water to baby brother, for my breasts are dry.

Mama, Mama, the killer birds are roaring in again!

Be brave, my love, be brave . . .

Mama, Mama, the giant firecrackers are here!

They are giant bombs and rockets.

They are coming, Mama! They are exploding!

Be brave, be brave, my little girl.

Mama, I'm scared.

Lovely, take your baby brother to a safer place after the killer birds have flown away.

And you, Mama?
What about you?
I'm scared, Mama.
Mama! Mama! Mama!
Don't die, Mama!
Don't leave us alone, Mama!
Sing to us, Mama, so that we may cry together.
Mama! Mama! Mama! Mama!

FAN YEW TENG
MALAYSIA

O God, Friend of the Poor

God friend of the poor help those of us who are rich
to bear the guilt and pain of our affluence.
The responsibility of riches takes too much of our time.
Guarding our riches gives us a siege mentality
and we have little energy left for others.
Forgive us Lord and help us to find a better, fairer way to live.

HAZEL DOWN
ENGLAND

Four lousy days per year,
Behind prison walls we visited.
Our mothers, our brothers
Our sisters our *whanau*,
We took the message of love.
We tried to make it moving,
By sharing personal feelings.

'*Tama ngakau marie*
Tama a te Atua.'

Son of peaceful heart
Son of God.

In spirit, in love we sang,
With action songs and dance.
Appealing to their Maoriness
Hopefully to touch their hearts.
'How can you lead our people,
We need your physical presence.
Stand tall – O Youth,
Regain your *mana*,
Reclaim your *wairua Maori*.
Stone walls become no barrier,
Claim Christ – He'll set you free
Just as you are, He'll take you now,
Accept him as a Maori.'

'What you are, is God's gift to you,
What you become, is your gift to God.'

MONA RIINI, TUHOE TRIBE
AOTEAROA NEW ZEALAND

On Friday afternoon, 18 March 1994, I was on my way to
Jucuapa, about half an hour drive west of San Miguel. Since
arriving back in El Salvador at the beginning of February I had
been working at the Baptist church in Jacuapa and making the
journey three or four times a week, sometimes more. A quick
and easy trip along the Pan-American Highway out of San
Miguel for about 20 miles and then two miles up a winding
country lane to Jucuapa, a sizeable town on a hill. Fridays had
become a regular day for going because I was leading a course
on worship for those responsible for conducting the services
on Sundays and during the week. Today was different though,
a group of us were going to an evangelical rally that another
church was holding in one of the nearby villages. I arranged to
pick folk up at three o'clock at the church. Cameron wanted to
come with me to play with David, the minister's son, but as he
had a lot of homework to do that day I went on my own.
Driving down a long hill before the turn-off for Jucuapa, a
silver jeep was tailing me. It followed me off the main road and
up the road to the town. After about a mile it overtook. We
passed some houses on either side and then its back door
opened and two men leapt out with shot-guns and ran towards
me. I jumped out of the car but they forced me back in and
made me lie, face down, in the back of the car. One of them
held a gun to my back, the other jumped in the driving seat and
swung the car round. We drove for about ten minutes. They
gave me my instructions – they would leave me somewhere, I
would have to wait for two hours before trying to get home, if I
left in less than two hours someone would kill me. I repeated
the instructions to them several times to make sure that I had
got it right. As soon as the car stopped I was told to jump out.
The man who had been in the back with me made an opening
in a hedge that led into a field. He shouted at me to run. I ran
down the field which sloped away from the road and jumped

into a ditch. I waited there for two and a half hours and then caught a bus back home.

JAMES GROTE
EL SALVADOR

God the Conqueror

The Exodus, with its picture of a God who takes the side of the oppressed and powerless, has been a beacon of hope for many in despair.

Yet, the liberationist picture of Yahweh is not complete. A delivered people is not a free people, nor is it a nation. People who have survived the nightmare of subjugation dream of escape. Once the victims have been delivered, they seek a new dream, a new goal, usually a place of safety away from the oppressors, a place that can be defended against future subjugation. Israel's new dream became the land of Canaan. And Yahweh was still with them: Yahweh promised to go before the people and give them Canaan, with its flowing milk and honey. The land, Yahweh decided, belonged to these former slaves from Egypt and Yahweh planned on giving it to them – using the same power used against the enslaving Egyptians to defeat the indigenous inhabitants of Canaan. Yahweh the deliverer became Yahweh the conqueror.

The obvious characters in the story for Native Americans to identify with are the Canaanites, the people who already lived in the promised land. As a member of the Osage Nation of American Indians who stands in solidarity with other tribal people around the world, I read the Exodus stories with Canaanite eyes. And, it is the Canaanite side of the story that has been overlooked by those seeking to articulate theologies of liberation. Especially ignored are those parts of the story that describe Yahweh's command to mercilessly annihilate the indigenous population.

ROBERT ALLEN WARRIOR

God of Freedom

God of freedom, God of justice
you whose love is strong as death,
you who saw the dark of prison,
you who knew the price of faith –
> touch our world of sad oppression
> with your Spirit's healing breath.

Rid the earth of torture's terror
you whose hands were nailed to wood;
hear the cries of pain and protest;
you who shed the tears and blood –
> move in us the power of pity
> restless for the common good.

Make in us a captive conscience
quick to hear, to act, to plead;
make us truly sisters, brothers
of whatever race or creed –
> teach us to be fully human,
> open to each other's needs.

(Tune: 'Rhuddlan'.)

SHIRLEY ERENA MURRAY
AOTEAROA NEW ZEALAND

'And Jesus looking upon him, loved him'
(Mark 10:21)

I picked red, shiny, firm strawberries for my table.
I ate as I picked
But I chose the small distorted ugly fruits.
I can't offer those.

I sit with bright, good looking friends.
I judged as I sat,
I didn't choose those that looked broken
I can't cope with problems.

Give me your heart, Lord.
Show me that the poor and broken
Are indeed blessed,
Just as the ugly fruit are sweet as nectar

LINDSAY REYNOLDS
ENGLAND

Mayan Prayer

God, beauty of the day, heart of the heavens and of the earth; giver of wealth, giver of daughters and of sons.

Help us to feel within ourselves the need to search for you, to invoke your name, to praise you along the roads, in the valleys, in the ravines, on the riverbanks, and under the trees.

Protect us, that we may not be entangled in evil, that we will not trip into shame and misfortune. Help us not to slip and get hurt, that we may not fall along the way. Protect us from obstacles that might pursue us or appear before us. Give us only beautiful straight paths, beautiful good paths.

Grant that we might believe in you, be drawn to you, and that our existence might be happy. O God, heart of the heavens and of the earth, hidden treasure. You fill the heavens and earth at the four cardinal points. Grant that there might be only

peace and tranquillity in the universe, before you, O God.
May it be so.

POPUL VUH MAYAN
ASIA

Meditation of Peace

Come with me on an imaginary journey. You may close your
eyes, but keep your ears, hearts, minds and spirit open. Relax
and enjoy this journey with me. Let's journey into the past –
the present – the future. Trust me.

There is darkness – total darkness – stillness – awesome
peace.

There is a faint thread of light piercing the darkness. There is
murmuring, movement, a heaving sense of unrest and heavy
breathing. There is a *hui* – debating – decision making –
warring . . . Then – there is struggling, grunting, groaning,
heaving, pushing – moaning with great pain.

As separation takes place, there is a *tangi,* wailing and
grieving as Rangi and Papa frantically struggle to cling to each
other. Papatuanuku cries in agony as the space between them
increases. Ranginui sheds tears of loneliness and grief . . . The
children rebel and go out into a new world, away from darkness into a world of light. They find their own domain yet still
maintain strong links with the rest. Some choose to remain
with Papa, while others join Rangi in the realms above and in
between them. One named Tane adorns Papa with native
bush, ferns, shrubs, birds and insects. – All is still now, quiet
and subdued.

Come, now. Here we are at the edge of a forest. Let us enter
into the forest, and enjoy the peace and tranquillity of the tall,
stately *totara,* the *miro,* the *tawa,* the *rewarewa.* The smaller
shrubs the vines, the clematis, the fernery, shelter under the
canopy of the taller trees, yet they retain their own individu-
ality, their stature, shape, size, colourful beauty. They stand
proud in their unity and earthly aroma of moss, earth and
dampness.

The nearby streams bubble over stones, and down little gorges – clear, cold, unpolluted fresh water – '*He wai Maori*'.

The bellbirds sing, the *tuis* sip the nectar from the *kowhai*, the fat *kereru* (pigeon) fly past to the nearest *miro*. The cheeky fantail challenges as it flits from branch to branch, within easy reach, yet quite evasive.

– Peace – tranquillity – serenity.

POPUL VUH MAYAN
ASIA

Hail to the Lord's Anointed

Hail to the Lord's Anointed
Great David's greater Son!
Hail, in the time appointed,
His reign on earth begun!
He comes to break oppression,
To set the captive free,
To take away transgression,
And rule in equity.

He comes with succour speedy
To those who suffer wrong;
To help the poor and needy,
And bid the weak be strong;
To give them songs for sighing,
Their darkness turns to light,
Whose souls, condemned and dying,
Were precious in his sight.

He shall come down like showers
Upon the fruitful earth;
And love, joy, hope, like flowers,
Spring in His path to birth:
Before Him, on the mountains,
Shall peace the herald go,
And righteousness in fountains
From hill to valley flow.

Kings shall fall down before him
And gold and incense bring;
And nations shall adore Him,
His praise all people sing;
For he shall have dominion
O'er river, sea, and shore,
Far as the eagle's pinion
Or dove's light wing can soar.

O'er every foe victorious,
He on His throne shall rest;
From age to age more glorious,
All-blessing and all blest:
The tide of time shall never
His covenant remove;
His name shall stand for ever;
That name to us is Love.

(Tune: Crüger.)

JAMES MONTGOMERY

THE OPTION FOR THE POOR

I decided that to be a Christian and a priest of the people, one has to take sides, to cast one's lot with the poor and oppressed . . . to be a Christian one must be prepared to be misunderstood, to be maligned and to be branded a 'subversive' . . . it is only when we start to feel and identify ourselves with others that we become alive.

MANNY LAHOZ
ASIA

In the months before we first left for El Salvador in August 1991 we often explained our reasons for going in terms of Christ's call to Peter, James and John in the Garden of Gethsemane to 'stay and keep watch' through the long night of suffering and on the edge of crucifixion. Christ was the suffering people of El Salvador on the edge of crucifixion in the midst of civil war and we, like the disciples, were being asked to do nothing more than to 'stay and keep watch' with them. Like many others we had done it from a distance in Britain, now we were being asked to move a little closer. 'Stay here and keep watch with me.' A call to solidarity, accompaniment. In the week before returning to Britain we explained our reason for leaving in terms of the same passage. The invitation and call of Jesus is met with severe limitations on the part of Peter, James and John. Exhausted and frightened by the events of the week they find themselves dozing and are caught doing so three times by Jesus. Like the disciples, we have had to admit our limitations in responding to the invitation and the call of Jesus and those who are suffering in El Salvador. The possibility of suffering another armed robbery in the future, more violent and more costly, is something that we couldn't live with or risk for us or the children. However willing the spirit was, the flesh was weak and we were frightened. The people around us who bid us farewell understood our fear – they had lived with the same sort of fear and violence, suspicion and uncertainty for many years and will continue to do so even in post civil war El Salvador. I think they also understood our limitations – that the cup of suffering is, in the end, theirs and not ours to drink. That is a fact which defines the limits of solidarity and accompaniment – as it did for Peter, James and John. Like them, it has been hard for us to admit to that.

JAMES GROTE
EL SALVADOR

It is cold
Get more cardboard friend

I am tired
Too bad friend you can't stop here

I am dirty
Too bad the public lavatories are locked for the night

I am hungry
Too bad friend there is no money

I need a friend
If only you knew that God loves you friend

But where is he?
He is here if you call friend

HAZEL DOWN
ENGLAND

The Hidden God

'Leave this chanting and singing and telling of beads. Who do you worship in this lonely dark corner of the temple with all the doors shut?

'Open your eyes and see that God is not in front of you.

'He is there where the farmer is tilling the hard ground and where the labourer is breaking stones. He is with them in the sun and the rain and his garment is covered with dust. Put off your holy cloak and like him come down on to the dusty soil.

'Deliverance? Where will you find deliverance? Our master himself has joyfully taken on the bonds of creation; he is bound with us for ever.

'Come out of your meditations and leave aside the flowers and the incense. What harm is there if your clothes become tattered and stained? Meet him and stand by him in toil and in the sweat of your brow.'

RABINDRANATH TAGORE
ASIA

Mary Song

What have you done to me? What have you made of me?
I cannot find myself in the woman you want me to be . . .
Haloed, alone . . . marble and stone: Safe, Gentle, Holy Mary.

My sisters, look at me! Don't turn in pain from me.
Your lives and mine are one in rage and agony . . .
Silenced, denied, or sanctified . . . Safe, Gentle, Holy Mary.

Revolution is my song! *Magnificat* proclaims it!
The promise that it makes to us, we dare now to reclaim it!
In our weakness we are strong: wise through pain and grief
　　　　and wrong . . .
Giving, loving, angry women.

All generations will acclaim me only if you can acclaim me . . .
Live with joy the truth you find – woman – this is what you
        name me:
Suffering, proud, prophetic, unbowed . . .
Whole, laughing, daughter . . . Mary:
Real, warm, living woman . . . Mary:
Then I will be *Wholly* Mary!

ANONYMOUS
ASIA

Extract from Communities of Freedom

The theme that fortnight was that Jesus was born poor and humble and shares our life, and the question was 'Why?' The women present were all poor. None had had much formal education. Most were migrants from rural areas. All knew real hardship. They could easily identify with a poor family on the move whose baby had been born in a stable. Indeed a one-minute reading of St Luke's account of the nativity provoked a one-hour discussion of the injustices, humiliations and hardships that the mothers themselves experienced.

They discussed the terrible health services available in the area and how a local woman's baby had been born while she was waiting in the queue to see the doctor (the baby died). They swapped accounts of having to wait in shops while better dressed people were served first and how as domestic servants they were treated without respect by their mistresses. They talked of the high price of food in the local shops . . .

'*Traditionally we have used the Bible as a window into the past. In the basic Christian communities, the Bible is held up as a mirror in which we see reflected our own lives.*'

After an hour the catechist put the question 'Why did Jesus choose to be born poor and humble?'

'Maybe,' said one woman, a mother of ten of whom three had died and only two were working, 'maybe it was to show these rich people that we are important too.'

A ripple of excitement went through the room. Was God really making such a statement about their humanity? About their rights as people? The discussion progressed, but with an electric charge in the air. Half an hour later, a young woman said, 'I think we still haven't got the right answer to the first question!' A complete hush. 'I think,' she went on, 'that God chose his Son to be born like us so that we can realise that we are important. It is not just to show the bosses. It's to show us too!'

And suddenly I saw what it means to say that the Gospel has the power to set people free, that the Good News to the poor is a message of liberation. For these women, fired by a sudden consciousness of their own worth, of their identification with Jesus Christ, by an awareness of God's love for them.

DEREK WINTER

Of Maize and Men

The wind sobs its way
over the scorched maize-fields,
greeting the peasants
in the bright shawls.

When our grandparents married
it was corncobs, corncobs all the way,
and the skies and the mountains
blessed their union.

Tall as a cornstalk
my son grows beside me,
and when it thunders he rests
his leaves against my side.

In the night hungry folk dream
of the grain that grows in the cornfields
and stroke their hungry brows
with their hands.

Of maize is my sadness,
of maize is my joy,
and when I dreamed I was wounded
a maizefield saved me.

Greater than the whole countryside
and all the earth's greenery,
is the man who with his kerchief
wipes the sweat from his brow.

The dead are born again
as maize seeds on the hillside
between the mouth of heaven
and the dove's beak.

I see God burgeoning
in the soil of the maizefields,
his hair the tall corn
waving in the wind.

In the fields at harvest-time
I see a greener life
and my feet find the path
that had been lost in the earth.

CARLOS CASTRO SAAVEDRA

The Devil and the Singer

(an old Filipino Folksong)

Devil: If you waste your time talking
to the people who don't listen
to the things that you are saying
who do you think is going to hear?

And if you should die explaining
how the things that they complain about
are things they could be changing
who do you think's going to hear?

There were other lonely singers
in a world turned deaf and blind,
who were crucified for what
they tried to show,
and their voices have been scattered
by the swirling winds of time
for the truth remains that
no-one wants to know

Singer: But you can still hear me singing
to the people who don't listen
to the things that I am saying
praying someone's going to hear,
and I guess I'll die explaining
how the things that they complain about
are the things they could be changing
hoping someone's going to care
'cause I don't believe that
no-one wants to know.

EXTRACT FROM *THE SMOULDERING LAND*
BY JULIAN EAGLE

God is on the side of the poor, the oppressed, the persecuted. When this faith is proclaimed and lived in a situation of political conflict between the rich and the poor, and when the rich and the powerful reject this faith and condemn it as heresy, we can read the signs and discern something more than a crisis. We are faced with a kairos, a moment of truth, a time for decision, a time of grace, a God-given opportunity for conversion and hope.

EXTRACT FROM *THE ROAD TO DAMASCUS*

PART THREE

Sing Magnificat

'I'm pore, I'm black, I may be ugly and can't cook, a voice say to everything listening. *But I'm here.*' With these words Celie, a black woman born in the Southern United States, brings to an end years of abuse and humiliation by her husband, in Alice Walker's novel, *The Color Purple* (The Women's Press, 1985, repr., p. 176). The love and support of other women give her the inner strength to leave the situation and to affirm herself. She is here; present; an undeniable reality.

The Color Purple's story of suffering, sisterhood, affirmation of self and of finding new community is the story of many women in our churches and societies, not least within the CWM family. In 1995, the United Nations International Year of Women, the suffering of women is still very much with us, as is reflected in the first contributions to this section. They speak of poverty, deprivation and discrimination. But it does not stop there. Like Celie in *The Color Purple*, many women in the world church have discovered their value and found new dignity – they too are created in the image of God. Some have found it through learning to listen to an inner voice (Margaret Schrader's contribution on spirituality); others through a new understanding of Jesus and the women and men that followed him ('Who is like Jesus?'). Vital in the process has been the support of others ('Affirmation: an idle tale').

Yet it still does not stop there. Self-affirmation, however important, needs to lead to seeking justice for others. From a position of strength, women worldwide have embraced the struggle for justice, peace and the integrity of creation.

Rosemary Ruether's self-blessing ritual leads to naming the forces of life and death, and in Kurinji Nathan's poem the hands which gently tend the leaves will work hard to weed out poverty and to show new ways for humankind. And that is the ultimate focus of this section and of women's struggles worldwide: a new community, when justice will be done for all, including the oppressor; when, in the words of Judy Chicago, both men and women will be gentle and both women and men will be strong; when everywhere will be called Eden once again.

Poverty, war, prejudice and family breakdown not only affect women – they are the daily reality of many children and young people in our world. 'My Mother's Name is Worry' is a poignant example of this. For young people the way that we deal with these issues is the ultimate test of faith – ours and their own. Many young people are not seeking 'catchphrase Christianity' ('A Journey of Questions') but a faith that sees the pain of people and seeks the wholeness of humankind. For some young people in the CWM family this search for faith with integrity has prompted them to apply for Training in Mission. This year-long programme brings together twelve people from different countries. They live, study and work together in mission projects in order to learn more about themselves, their faith and the church's role in God's mission. Some of their experiences can be found in this section.

The former TIM-participants and many others are proof that young people are much more than 'the future of the church'. They are here now and they form a rich resource: they bring their own unique understanding of faith and interpretation of the Gospel. More importantly, they come with their own vision of a better world in which people will live together in a new way. That should not surprise us. It was an Old Testament prophet who long ago spoke of young people daring to dream.

FRANCIS BRIENEN

SUFFERING WOMEN

– all she had to live on (Luke 21:4)

She sold gloves at our garden gate;
the wool from old jumpers.
But how much of a market
was there for woolly gloves
in that heat?
My fingers fumbled the latch
and my ears strained
for a language foreign to me.
As our eyes met I thought
what can I do about
widowhood and hungry children?
What difference can I make
to the weight of indignity
and the pain of injustice?
I bought some gloves.
A month later
she was back at my gate
with two pairs for the baby.
The following month
a large pair in mustard yellow
for *mfundisi*.*
Her story became knitted into mine:
I cannot cast her off.
We're no longer there
so who buys the gloves now?

Stitching Spirit,
pull us together
into your vital pattern
that will not unravel with indifference

*A Zulu word meaning 'minister'.

or fray with neglect:
to which each contributes
all we have so that together
we may live on.

JANET LEES, *REFLECTIONS ON
SOUTH AFRICA*
ENGLAND

Prayer of a Harassed Mum

Oh where, oh where do I find you?
My life is filled with pressure,
'starving' kids, unpaid bills.
The tears run down,
no one is there to comfort.
When life is dark and there's no way out,
when 'starving' kids are filled,
You Lord, are here
with everlasting arms to enfold and comfort.

JO NEWHAM
ENGLAND

To Kang Duk Kyung*

Downcast lids
Curtaining pain

Wrinkled skin
Enfolding shame

Inscrutable face
Hidden agony.

Why you and not I?
Will I ever comprehend?

I can never
Stand in your place.

Sing Magnificat   91

So,
I take your hand
Feel the breath of your sigh
Hear deep rivers in your voice
Dark gorges of anger
Deep ravines of heartache
Tall cliffs of strength
Echoing . . . re-echoing

'I have survived!'

*A former 'comfort woman', aged 64 years.

RANJINI REBERA
ASIA

A Woman's Experience

I am taking part in an ecumenical conference. In my working group are eleven high ranking men and myself, a laywoman.

I am politely asked what I expect from the conference. I say that for me a *new* community of women and men in the church is important.

'Madam,' replied the Metropolitan, 'I did not come here to talk about problems relating to women.'

'Madam,' the bishop informs me, 'women have an important task and it is to educate their sons so that they become priests.'

'Madam,' says another bishop angrily, 'do you not realise that Protestant women are destroying the ecumenical movement?'

The cardinal says nothing about this matter.

The moderator – striving to be civil – closes the subject: 'Madam, I do not understand women – they hate men, you know!'

With difficulty I keep my composure!

Next day at a reception – I have a glass of blueberry jelly in my hand – the moderator speaks to me once again: 'So what then is women's spirituality, tell me?'

I try to explain and remind him of a woman with the ointment who expressed her faith and her love in a way which was wholly her own. My hands try to help me explain – and the blueberry jelly spills all over my dress.

That ends the conversation.

The toilet attendant tries to console me. She cannot know that I am not crying over my dress.

CONFERENCE OF EUROPEAN CHURCHES (CEC)

Traditions

The cobra can bite and pour out poison,
The scorpion can sting and create fear,
But God who created female and male
In his image, had not given any such defensive instrument to
      women.
Child bearing, caring and nurturing weakens her physically
      year after year.
Is her physical weakness a tool to exploit her and incur on her
      shameful deeds?
When this continues day after day
Where is the hope?

Where is the hope when one sees
the struggles of the woman
in the villages and slums?
Is there literacy
so they can read and learn and
understand? – No.
Is there land to till
and so come out of economic
struggles? – No.
Is there anything? –
Nothing – Nothing – Nothing at all.
How will the millions of women come out of the gutters to
      take up equal partnership?

So what to do? What to do?
It is the tradition that a woman should be tied to a man
        sometime in her life.
Even if a man batters, kicks and kills her,
woman cannot break that tradition.
A woman buys the man with cash, gold and immovable
        property.
That is the tradition.
But the male bought by the female
forgets that he is a slave
and lords it over the mistress.
Society accepts it; society supports it.
It wants to flourish with the hard earned money of the woman.
Where is the rationale in that?
But that is the tradition.
Indians are highly intellectual.

It is the tradition.
Indian traditions are higher then Everest in the Himalayas,
stronger than any modern machine in the world.

May the Good Lord, Creator of all things
change histories, break traditions,
bring forth new orders
and give everlasting strength and patience,
to women who continue to struggle and strive
Till a New Community of women and men is built
To bring glory to him.

SUGUNA DEVASUNDERAM
INDIA

Story of a Mother of Triplets

Economic growth and modernisation, glaring highrise buildings and displays of fashion all demonstrate the contemporary success story of Korea. In the shadow of this phenomenon are stories of tragedy and despair.

Ms Choi Yun-Ho was born in 1960 into a poor family. She grew up with a drunken and violent father and never ceasing family quarrels. She ran away from home and married a young man who was slightly disabled. As a textile worker she earned a meagre income which barely supported her and her family.

When the triplets were born, her first worry was how she was going to feed these three beautiful children. Their one-room house was too small for the family and the landlords did not want crying babies around. They moved to an illegal squat on a hillside. After a while they decided to build a bigger shelter. As they were digging on a nearby hill, a fire destroyed the squat with the children inside.

When the grief-stricken mother was spreading the children's ashes some nursery teachers came forward to console her. She said to them, 'Why did you not come sooner? Where we lived there was no nursery and while we were preparing a new shelter I had to leave my children locked inside the squat.'

Of course, without her children it would have been easy for the mother to move away. Yet she stayed and is now working in the nursery which was built in memory of the deceased triplets.

SUN AI LEE PARK
KOREA

Woman

I am a woman, a woman am I,
Created by God, a part of man,
I was created to change the world.
One among many,
Blessed by God with the gift
To conceive the human race,
I gave birth in pain.
So much pain, pain,
Over and over again.
I bear many strains
To increase the human race.
Blood of my blood,
flesh of my flesh,
So that man and woman
shall always inhabit the earth.
Without me children will
cease to be born.
United with man,
I am an important part
of the master's plan.

I am a companion, friend
mother, lover,
A burden bearer,
A burden sharer,
A nurse, teacher,
homemaker, to keep the home together,
A leader,
A radiant light.
I am uniquely made.
A wonderful and blessed creation.

JULIET MORIAH
GUYANA

God
Who created
Woman and man
To bear your image
And share your glory;
And through
A woman and a man
Defeated all defeat
And set us free;
Renew in us
The faith of Mary,
The love of Jesus
And the joy of all
The saints;
That the creatures
Of the earth
May sing your praise
For evermore. Amen.

ANGELA TILBY
ENGLAND

There is a woman who is tired of acting weak
when she knows she is strong,
and there is a man who is tired of appearing strong
when he feels vulnerable.

There is a woman who is tired of acting humble,
and there is a man who is burdened with the constant
expectation of knowing everything.

There is a woman who is tired of being called 'an emotional
        female',
and there is a man who is denied
the right to be weak and to be gentle.

There is a woman who is called unfeminine when she
        competes,
and there is a man for whom competition is
the only way to prove his masculinity.

There is a woman who is tired of being a sex object,
and there is a man who must worry about his potency.

There is a woman who feels 'tied down' by her children,
and there is a man who is denied the full pleasure of shared
        parenthood.

There is a woman who is denied meaningful employment or
        equal pay,
and there is a man who must bear full
financial responsibility for another human being.

Bringing the promise of New Community,
there is a woman who takes a step toward her own liberation,
and there is a man who finds the way to freedom is made a
        little easier.

BETTY THOMPSON

Prayer from Korea

In the beginning God was. In the beginning God, who is the origin of everything, existed with the moaning of women, with the women giving birth, with the poor women and with the weak women. God, who created everything for good, existed with those women who were created in God's image.

FROM A LITURGY OF KOREAN CHURCH WOMEN UNITED

'I spend much of my days reflecting with women on their relationship to God. Some come to my home and place of work, The Still Point, just to do that. Others come as a result of pain in their life. Many of these are women who have been abused by people within the church, some of whom are clergy.

'As I reflect on my journey and theirs, I begin to see some patterns emerging as we journey ever more deeply into our own reality and into the reality that is God.

'The first is the movement of being aware of God as 'out there' or 'up there' to God within. It is a recognition of the sacredness of our own lives, and indeed our own bodies. It is a recognition that God speaks not only through the Bible, the church and other authority figures, but also through our feelings, our intuition and in that deep quiet voice within each one of us.

'Many of us take a long while to trust that inner voice.'

MARGARET SCHRADER
AOTEAROA NEW ZEALAND

An Idle Tale

When our sister is ignored, ridiculed –
so that her concerns need not be heard:

> *We shall tell an idle tale*
> *of resurrection power.*

When our sister is harassed, dehumanised –
and her protests labelled 'a fuss about nothing':

> *We shall tell an idle tale*
> *of resurrection power.*

When our sister is abused, raped –
and then accused of 'asking for it':

> *We shall tell an idle tale*
> *of resurrection power.*

When our sister is beaten, brutalised –
so that she can barely raise her head:

> *We shall tell an idle tale*
> *of resurrection power.*

When our sisters discover their value –
despite their humiliations:

> *We shall sing Magnificat*
> *and know the truth of Easter.*

When our sisters grow tall and walk together –
unnerving the powerful with their dignity:

> *We shall sing Magnificat*
> *and know the truth of Easter.*

When our sisters tell their idle tale –
and are believed and honoured:

> *We shall sing Magnificat*
> *and know the truth of Easter.*

When our sisters know God within them –
and see their natures affirmed in Hers:

> *We shall sing Magnificat*
> *and know the truth of Easter.*

KATE COMPSTON
ENGLAND

Litany of Mary of Nazareth

For this litany, the congregation is to be divided into two groups.

Group 1: Glory to you, God our creator.
  Group 2: **Breathe into us new life, new meaning.**

Group 1: Glory to you, God our saviour.
  Group 2: **Lead us into the way of peace and justice.**

Group 1: Glory to you, healing Spirit.
  Group 2: **Transform us to empower others.**

Group 1: Mary, wellspring of peace
  Group 2: **Be our guide.**
Group 1: Model of strength
  Group 2: **Be our guide.**
Group 1: Model of gentleness
  Group 2: **Be our guide.**
Group 1: Model of trust
  Group 2: **Be our guide.**
Group 1: Model of courage
  Group 2: **Be our guide.**
Group 1: Model of patience
  Group 2: **Be our guide.**
Group 1: Model of risk
  Group 2: **Be our guide.**
Group 1: Model of openness
  Group 2: **Be our guide.**

Group 1: Model of perseverance
    Group 2: **Be our guide.**

Group 2: Mother of the liberator
    Group 1: **Pray for us.**
Group 2: Mother of the homeless
    Group 1: **Pray for us.**
Group 2: Mother of the dying
    Group 1: **Pray for us.**
Group 2: Mother of the non-violent
    Group 1: **Pray for us.**
Group 2: Widowed mother
    Group 1: **Pray for us.**
Group 2: Unwed mother
    Group 1: **Pray for us.**
Group 2: Mother of a political prisoner
    Group 1: **Pray for us.**
Group 2: Mother of the condemned
    Group 1: **Pray for us.**

Group 1: Oppressed woman
    Group 2: **Lead us to life.**
Group 1: Liberator of the oppressed
    Group 2: **Lead us to life.**
Group 1: Marginalised woman
    Group 2: **Lead us to life.**
Group 1: Comforter of the afflicted
    Group 2: **Lead us to life.**
Group 1: Cause of our joy
    Group 2: **Lead us to life.**
Group 1: Sign of contradiction
    Group 2: **Lead us to life.**
Group 1: Breaker of bondage
    Group 2: **Lead us to life.**
Group 1: Political refugee
    Group 2: **Lead us to life.**
Group 1: Seeker of sanctuary
    Group 2: **Lead us to life.**

Group 1: First disciple
    Group 2: **Lead us to life.**
Group 1: Sharer in Christ's passion
    Group 2: **Lead us to life.**
Group 1: Seeker of God's will
    Group 2: **Lead us to life.**
Group 1: Witness to Christ's resurrection
    Group 2: **Lead us to life.**

Group 2: Woman of mercy
    Group 1: **Empower us.**
Group 2: Woman of faith
    Group 1: **Empower us.**
Group 2: Woman of contemplation
    Group 1: **Empower us.**
Group 2: Woman of vision
    Group 1: **Empower us.**
Group 2: Woman of wisdom and understanding
    Group 1: **Empower us.**
Group 2: Woman of grace and truth
    Group 1: **Empower us.**
Group 2: Woman, pregnant with hope
    Group 1: **Empower us.**
Group 2: Woman centred on God
    Group 1: **Empower us.**

IN GOD'S IMAGE
ASIA

Who is like Jesus?

Who is like Jesus?
Jesus talked with a Samaritan woman.
He took water from an outcast woman.
Are you like him?
Won't you do like Jesus?

Who is like Jesus?
Jesus forgave the prostitute woman.
He gave justice to the sinner.
Are you like him?
Won't you do like Jesus?

Who is like Jesus?
Jesus taught the word of God to Mary a woman.
He made known to her the love of God.
Are you like him?
Won't you do like Jesus?

Who is like Jesus?
Jesus was touched by the unclean woman.
He healed the woman who was bleeding.
Are you like him?
Won't you do like Jesus?

Who is like Jesus?
Jesus consoled the widow from Nain.
He wiped her tears away.
Are you like him?
Won't you do like Jesus?

Who is like Jesus?
Jesus appreciated the widow at the temple.
He paid attention to a poor woman.
Are you like him?
Won't you do like Jesus?

Who is like Jesus?
Jesus liberated the woman who was bent over.
He gave her health and happiness.

Are you like him?
Won't you do like Jesus?

Who is like Jesus?
Jesus took women in his ministry.
He called them to follow him.
Are you like him?
Won't you do like Jesus?

Who is like Jesus?
Jesus comforted the women at the tomb.
He commanded them to preach the Gospel.
Are you like him?
Won't you do like Jesus?

IVALEEN AMANNA
INDIA

Women of the Way (Luke 8:1–3)

How did you gather the courage to go
leaving home
husband
father and mother?

Did your father ever speak to you again, Susanna?
or were you as one dead to him
throwing the family's reputation
– never mind about yours –
to the wind
by going on the road
with a bunch of men?

What did your mother say, Joanna?
or did she say nothing
lips pursed in a tight mouth
in that familiar way you knew meant
she was deeply disapproving
but would not speak

Maybe you had the easier part, Mary
for your demons had given you
the label
mad
eccentric
maybe you no longer had a family
who called you theirs
        or did they wish
        now you were healed,
        sane and whole
        that you would stay
        to finally be the daughter
        you could never be before?

But the three of you left home
and went with him
you had each other
and the other, nameless, women too

Can you tell us what the men thought?
Mark and Matthew
Judas, Thaddeus
Bartholomew and the rest
(we know their names)

how did they cope with
Jesus' easy manner with you
the way he welcomed your presence
as he said the things
a rabbi entrusts only to his closest disciples?

did they expect it was an infatuation
only lasting for a week or two
that the rigours of the road
would prove too much for women?

as you stayed with them,
and days turned into weeks, then months
did they finally accept
you would continue

following
supporting
ministering?

disciples by decision – like them

disciples by deed – like them

disciples to the death

SUSAN JONES
AOTEAROA NEW ZEALAND

Tomorrow is Ours

We live without living
We die without dying
And yet . . .
We dare to dream
We dare to believe
We dare to hope
In a new day – tomorrow
For we know
That we are power.

FROM READING THE BIBLE
AS ASIAN WOMEN
1987 CHRISTIAN
CONFERENCE OF ASIA

Self-blessing ritual

(As each blessing is invoked, everyone touches the part of the body being mentioned.)

All:

In blessing our foreheads
We claim the power of reason.

In blessing our eyes
We claim the power of vision,
    to see clearly the forces
    of life and death in our midst.

In blessing our lips
We claim the power to speak the truth
    about our experiences,
We claim the power to name.

In blessing our hands
We claim our powers as artisans
    of a new humanity.

Women only:

In blessing our wombs
We claim the power to give birth,
    as well as the power
    to choose not to give birth.

All:

In blessing our feet
We claim the power to walk the path
    of our courageous foremothers
And when necessary to forge new paths.

All join hands:

In blessing each other,
We claim the power that rests collectively
    in our shared struggle as women and men.

ADAPTED FROM *RITE OF NAMING* BY
ROSEMARY RADFORD RUETHER
PHILIPPINES

Come and show us how to serve the refugees and the
    oppressed;
how to stand alongside those who struggle for social justice
and for the human rights of women and young people.
Come, liberate us from captivity to confessionalism,
and make us agents of reconciliation and unity.
Give us a will to live and serve you
through loving and serving others.
Keep us from insisting upon our own way.
Show us your way.
Enable us to grow in the knowledge of your truth.
Make us bearers of hope, and instruments of peace.
May we be living witnesses of that unity
which binds Divine Parent, Son and Holy Spirit
into one forgiving and redeeming God.

WOMEN STUDENTS IN THE PAN-AFRICAN
LEADERSHIP COURSE
ZAMBIA

The hands which gently tend the leaves
Will now help to banish darkness;
They'll work hard to put down evil,
And to raise up for all, new life.
The hands which gently tend the leaves
Will nourish all that is good;
They'll work hard to weed out poverty,
And bring in new culture and art.
The hands which gently tend the leaves
Will show new ways for humankind;
They'll work hard to build those structures
In which truth and right will be found.

KURINJI NATHAN
SRI LANKA

Exodus

The Israelites walked through the sea on dry ground. But when the Egyptian chariots with their horses and drivers went into the sea, the Lord brought the water back, and it covered them. The prophet Miriam, Aaron's sister, took her tambourine, and all the women followed her, playing tambourines and dancing. Miriam sang for them: 'Sing to the Lord, because he has won a glorious victory; he has thrown the horses and their riders into the sea' (Exodus 15:19–21).

In vibrant celebration
  women dance
  waters dance
celebrating
  community in sisterhood
  solidarity in liberation.

Water is Life
women birth Life
  Let us celebrate Life
  God's gift of liberation!

RANJINI REBERA
AUSTRALIA

Of Women and of Women's Hopes we sing

Of women and of women's hopes we sing:
of sharing in creation's nurturing,
of bearing and of birthing new belief,
of passion for the promise of life.

We praise the God whose image is our own,
the mystery within our flesh and bone,
the womanspirit moving through all time
in prophecy, Magnificat and dream.

We labour for the commonwealth of God
and, equal as disciples, walk the road,
in work and status, asking what is just,
for sisters of the family of Christ.

Forgiving what is past, we seek the new:
a finer justice, and a peace more true,
the promise of empowering for our day
when men and women roll the stone away.

SHIRLEY ERENA MURRAY AND JANE
MARSHALL
AOTEAROA NEW ZEALAND AND USA

Singing for our lives

We are a gentle, loving people and
we are singing, singing for our lives
We are buildings of New Creation and
we are singing, singing for our lives
We are the community-seeking women and
we are sharing, sharing our own lives
We are the owners of our body and
we are affirming, affirming our lives
We are the commitment-making women and
we are loving, loving in our lives
We are the tradition-changing women and
we are singing, singing for our lives
We are the language-conscious women and
we are speaking, speaking for our lives.

FROM READING THE BIBLE AS ASIAN WOMEN,
CHRISTIAN CONFERENCE OF ASIA

And then all that has divided us will merge
And then compassion will be wedded to power
And then softness will come to a world that is harsh and
         unkind
And then both men and women will be gentle
And then both women and men will be strong
And then no person will be subject to another's will
And then all will be rich and free and varied
And then the greed of some will give way to the needs of many
And then all will share equally in the Earth's abundance
And then all will care for the sick and the weak and the old
And then all will nourish the young
And then all will cherish life's creatures
And then all will live in harmony with each other and the
         Earth
And then everywhere will be called Eden once again.

JUDY CHICAGO

SUFFERING YOUNG PEOPLE

My Mother's Name is Worry

My mother's name is worry
In summer, my mother worries about water,
In winter, she worries about coal briquettes,
And all year long, she worries about rice.

In daytime, my mother worries about living,
At night, she worries for children.
And all day long, she worries and worries.

Then my mother's name is worry,
My father's is drunken frenzy,
And mine is tears and sighs.

A TWELVE-YEAR-OLD CHILD IN A SLUM AREA
ASIA

What did you do in South Africa, mummy?

What did you do in South Africa, mummy?

I watched children die
>of leukaemia,
>a first world disease,
>and kwashiorkor,
>a third world disease,
>side by side

>by drowning
>in a township river,
>when a municipal pool
>stayed empty

>in a road accident,
>as a fast car
>cut a corner

>from bullet wounds

in shacks and squatter camps,
where the sound of AK47s
punctuated the night.

What did you mourn in South Africa, mummy?

I mourned child victims
>of crises
>in cells and bodies
>as care and technology
>strove to sustain life

>of inequalities
>in health care
>and civic spending,
>that put hospital beds
>and swimming pools
>out of bounds

>of human carelessness,
>and a view
>that some life
>comes cheap

>of political power struggles
>and unwelcomed attempts
>to create a new era
>with a bullet or a bomb.

What did you pray for in South Africa, mummy?

I prayed that children might live
>where sharing resources
>leads to justice,
>caring and technology
>create health,
>prophetic leadership
>gives birth to peace,
>building reconciliation
>gives rise to hope –
>the tasks of the whole community:
>where love fuels new life.

In memory of all the children who have died on the road to the new South Africa.

JANET LEES
ENGLAND AND SOUTH AFRICA

Domingo Claudio, ten years old

Domingo now lives at Luanda airport. He makes his living by gathering rice that is spilled during the unloading of food from relief flights. He sells the rice to market vendors.

'I'm my mother's eldest son. I had a little brother, but he was hit by a bullet during the fighting and he died. Now I'm all alone. My mother was already an invalid and she was killed by UNITA.

'If you go up to someone's house, they call you a thief. And I'm not a thief. But even if you're not a thief, they accuse you of being one. Many people call us street urchins, walking the streets in dirty clothes and begging.

'Some people say, "Look at this vermin." And I say, "You know nothing. What are you talking about?" And I walk away. Sometimes you meet people who hit you and I say, "What have I done?" But that makes them even angrier. And they start beating you again. You have to keep quiet. You're hurt and only God knows about it. That's how it is. I hope someone can take me away from the airport. Even if it's just for the weekend. I wouldn't have to sleep in the streets and be killed by bandits.

'I think about a lot of things. I'd like to live in a house and be free. I'd like to live somewhere where I wouldn't have to fight with the others. Where I could play with friends. Where I could have a bath, wander around, watch TV. And after watching TV, go and play. Then go to sleep and the next day, play again. Do the washing up and clean the house. And after that, I'd play on the veranda with my own toys. That's what I'd like.'

FROM *ENCOUNTERS: LOST CHILDREN OF ANGOLA*

Goodbye, Mom and Dad

Ms Kwon stands before the dead bodies of her three daughters. The girls have left the family with a hope for happiness for Jaeman, their brother. No more will they cause concern to the poor and struggling family.

Ms Kwon's story is common in many Asian communities, both rural and urban. She has given birth to girls, a pity for everyone in the family. In order to have 'a boy please' she has ended up with four daughters.

The girls gradually discovered they were considered a bad omen and the root cause of the problems the family was encountering. It took them little time to decide that the solution to all problems was to end their own lives.

Ms Kwon's daughters are the victims of a society where women cannot maintain their human dignity and worth.

HAROLD WILLIAMS
ASIA

The apartheid of gender is the cruellest and the most pervasive discrimination of all, yet it has not yet generated a sustained condemnation on a global scale. More than a million girls die each year simply because they are born female. If the new world order is to usher in a just world, then this apartheid of gender too must go. And for that to happen, girls' education must be seen as a critical empowering tool.

JAMES P. GRANT

Hallo God, is that you?

Last week in Sunday School the teacher said we should talk to
you like we phone up our friends – so here goes –
   In our house there is not much privacy so when my Mum
and Dad have a quarrel, I can't help hearing. What was it like in
Nazareth? Perhaps Mary and Joseph never quarrelled. I want
to say to my parents – 'Don't quarrel, cuddle each other.' But
it's difficult, God. Could you do something about it, please?
   There is a girl at school whose parents have split up. Could
you help her and her parents? I expect you know how awful it
is for the children.
   Amen.

RITA DALGLEISH
ENGLAND

Our Hope

Our hope's for unification,
Even in sleeping it is our dream.
We offer even our lives
For the unity of our land.
Come to us, unification!
All people in this land wait for you,
Come now and heal our division
Unification come!

POPULAR LIBERATION SONG
AMONG THE YOUTH MOVEMENT
IN SOUTH KOREA

A Journey of Questions

Christian questions question Christians,
so Christians shy away from questions.
Catchphrase Christians carry answers:
The–Son–Of–God–Saves–Sinners–Amen
. . . the cow jumped over the moon.

Jesus had a life to live:
loving, hating, eating, sleeping, dying (rising).
So a boy from Birmingham joins a Jew from Nazareth
on a journey of questions.
Don't worry about answers, keep asking 'why?'

EDWARD COX
ENGLAND

A Plea to Us

*'You will always have the poor people with you, and any time you want
to, you can help them' (Mark 14:7).*
If Jesus said the poor will always be with us, what can we do
about it? What's the point of striving to affect something that is
going to remain with us?

He also said, 'Any time you want to you can help them.' No
use struggling and saying, 'It's too big a problem.'

Or 'I can't do anything about it.'

Because you *can*.

A smile and a cup of tea for a homeless person outside your
office.

Ten pounds to Rwanda – life-saving treatment for cholera
victims.

You'd feel pretty good if you saved a drowning child in a
swimming pool. A tenner will save dozens of children in
Rwanda.

You see, anytime you want to, you can help them.
But do you *want* to?

SIMON BOUND
ENGLAND

Story of Harriet and the cycling tour

My name is Harriet and I'm from the Netherlands. I live in a small town in the province of Brabant. I am 17 years old and I go to secondary school. I don't know yet what I will do afterwards. I am a Catholic, but I don't go to church very often. In my church you don't see many young people. Last year I spent my summer holidays in a rather special way. I participated in a bicycle tour organised by *Mission and Youth*.

Mission and Youth is a Roman Catholic foundation which tries to involve young people in mission. They understand mission as 'breaking through frontiers within yourself and society'. The bicycle tour lasted two weeks. In a group of young people, not only Catholics, I cycled through my own province. We met many different people on the road. One of them was Sister Ria, who works in a small home for people who have become homeless. The people living in the home are in some kind of crisis situation. What struck me was their vulnerability. They don't have family or friends to rely on. Often they experience problems which started in their youth. I asked myself: 'Why them and not me?' I felt so privileged. We also met people who formed some kind of community. They live according to Gandhi's principles of non-violence, simplicity, working with your hands and wholeness in action and reflection. Meeting them made me think about the choices that I want to make in my life. The bicycle tour has been very important to me. It has started a process of trying to find out what the Christian faith really means to me.

EGBERT VAN DER STOUW
THE NETHERLANDS

An Encounter in Jamaica

The Training in Mission programme has been the most difficult, challenging and valuable thing I have ever done. For one year our group of ten lived, learned, studied, argued, played, laughed and struggled together in order to learn about the mission of God.

During the final three months of the programme I was part of a Mission-Extension-Renewal-Impact-Team (MERIT) in Jamaica. The MERIT programme runs for approximately three months in a church community which has no minister. The idea is for the team to identify people to whom they can pass on their skills and ideas so that the church community can continue growing when the team moves out. The secret is to work *with* the people and not for the people. Our main focus was on the young people and young adults in the area.

One day we visited a 15 year old girl hoping that she could introduce us to other young people; we intended to start a youth fellowship. We walked around the streets and spoke to several young men. One told us he was just off to play cricket with his mates so we invited ourselves along.

When we arrived there were about; 20 young men aged between 16–20. It had started to rain a little and so they were sheltering inside a partly built house with only half a roof. When they heard we were missionaries they decided to make a quick exit but we blocked the doorways so they had to listen to what we had to say!

We told them what we were doing and they asked us what we could do for them. We replied that the question was really what they could do for themselves with our assistance. After a while we ran out of things to say and an awkward pause told us it was time to leave. So we made our excuses and promised to return later.

At that moment a thunder storm began, the rain didn't just fall – it plummeted! I was trying to put on a brave smile but I was pretty scared!

Some of the young men were visibly frightened and were leaning against the wall farthest away from the half open roof.

One of them suggested that we pray. We were a little surprised by the request but we happily obliged and asked them all to stand in a circle and hold hands. I think they surprised themselves a bit by doing it! We prayed for our safety and that of our families through the storm.

When we finished their attitude towards us had changed completely. They started talking about themselves and asked us questions too. One of them asked if we could sing together, so we sang some choruses. Eventually, our transport arrived to take us back home but the lads made us promise to return.

On reflection I can conclude only one thing. God sent the storm to help us break the ice with those young men. That evening, after returning home, we prayed together giving thanks to God for our time together with them and especially for that lovely storm!

LIZ BAKER
ENGLAND/JAMAICA

The Training in Mission Creed

As Training in Mission participants:

We acknowledge the faith journeys of past TIM groups as paving the way and laying the foundation for our own faith journey.

We believe that within our rich diversity of different races, characteristics and beliefs, different cultures and traditions and different gifts to share, we are one people out of many peoples; we can understand ourselves by understanding each other.

We believe in the Trinity which transcends the diversity of its expression; in the Creator God who made humanity live in harmony with the whole creation; in Jesus Christ, our saviour, who redeemed us from sin and liberates us from all oppression; and in the Holy Spirit who renews all creation and enables our involvement in God's mission.

We believe that the Trinity calls the Church to cross-cultural partnership as the Body of Christ; ours is an expression of unity in living together; through friendship and fellowship, devotion and worship we discover and experience our oneness in the spirit of 'koinonia' [partnership].

We believe that we are called to ecumenical engagement in God's mission through active participation and prayerful reflection. We believe that mission in Christ's way is the central role of the church in order to extend the Kingdom of God on earth, as it is in heaven.

In all this we believe, for we have experienced it!

FROM *TRAINING IN MISSION* 1992–93

Prayer for Youth Sunday

We have seen pain – pain of people in need;
People who suffer because there is no peace or justice.
Yet we see signs of hope too –
Hope in the missions, the churches, the individuals
Who seek the wholeness of humankind.
We give thanks to you, Lord, for opportunities to see and
       experience
The pain and hope of others.
We pray that we may commit ourselves
To share their sufferings, their pain –
And work towards God's justice
Bringing hope to all.
Lord, in your mercy, hear our prayer. Amen.

COUNCIL FOR MISSION AND ECUMENICAL CO-OPERATION
AOTEAROA NEW ZEALAND

The Earth is the Lord's
(based on Psalm 24)

Hey man! Everything belongs to God.
And don't you dare go around abusing it.
For you are responsible and accountable
for all that has been created.

Hey man! You are expected to live right
with all that has been created.
That means, being sensible and responsible
in everything you do.

Hey man! Rejoice and be happy in the
fellowship with God Almighty!!!

YOUTH IN MISSION WORKCAMP
NAURU, CENTRAL PACIFIC

The Lord's Prayer

Dearest Father who lives in heaven,
may your name be kept pure
Let peace reign and let everyone be equal
on earth as well as in heaven
Provide us with our daily needs as well as our spiritual needs
Please forgive us the things we have done wrong
as we will forget the bad things others have done to us
Help us not to be tempted to hurt you
and keep Satan away from us
Because you made the earth and heaven and everything in it
and you are all powerful and we should give you glory
through all eternity.
We all agree with this!

CHILDREN'S CAMP (AGED EIGHT TO FOURTEEN)
NORTH INDIA

Prayer for Youth

Mother and Father God,
You see and know the hearts of all your children.
Guide those of us who have strayed from your path of
        righteousness.
Have compassion, O Lord, and bring us back safely to your
        fold.
Help us to remember you now in the days of our youth.
Let us not wait until we are old.
Help those of us who already know you personally
to bring our brothers and our sisters to you also.
These mercies we ask in your precious name, O Lord.

OMODELE CRAIG
GUYANA

A Child asked me

A child asked me:
'What's this paper for?'
'For you to tell God
what you're sorry about,'
I replied, adding
'You can write it or draw.'
'I'll do both,' she said
and, borrowing my pen,
quickly drew a figure
and began to write.
'How do you spell people?'
she asked me –
direct and matter of fact
as if writing to God
was a daily task
hindered only by spelling.
Her question answered
she placed the folded paper
in the basket
with all the others.

Dear God,
I'm sorry.
Help me love people.

JANET LEES
ENGLAND/SOUTH AFRICA

Love
(based on 1 Corinthians 13)

Love is a whisper,
Not a tornado.
Love is a drift of petals,
Not a mighty oak tree,
Love is the song of a flute,
Not the blast of a trumpet.

Love is a beckoning finger,
Not a pair of handcuffs.
This is its strength.
It invites,
It does not force.
It's like a camp fire.
We gather round,
And are warmed.

ANNA COMPSTON, AGED TWELVE
ENGLAND

Il y a de l'espérance

Il y a de l'espérance pour mon avenir
Sa Parole, Ses Promesses vont s'accomplir
Il tient ma vie entre Ses Mains
Je n'ai rien à craindre pour mon demain.

> Il ne ment pas
> Il ne change pas
> Il est toujours là
> Suffisant pour moi

Il y a de l'espérance pour mon avenir
Sa Parole, Ses Promesses vont s'accomplir
Il tient ma vie entre Ses Mains
Je n'ai rien à craindre pour mon demain.

> Il est vivant
> Il est Tout Puissant
> Il est Présent
> Plus que Suffisant!

Translation: There is hope

There is hope for my future
His Word, his Promises will come true
He holds my life in his hands
I have nothing to fear for my tomorrow

> He does not lie
> He does not change
> He is always there
> Enough for me

There is hope for my future
His Word, his Promises will come true
He holds my life in his hands
I have nothing to fear for my tomorrow

> He is alive
> He is all powerful
> He is present
> More than enough.

HANTA RAMAKAVELO
MADAGASCAR

Hope for the Children

Hope for the children in our midst,
facing a world that's conflict torn.
All that they ask is time to grow,
and live the years for which they're born.

Hope for the children ev'rywhere,
we'll build with them a world of peace.

Rumours of war sound ev'rywhere,
wondering if there's a chance for peace.
Yet for all children that we love,
we will not yield 'til hate shall cease.

Peace is the goal of all we do.
Love leads to justice on the earth.
Let justice flow like waters clear,
so we may see the world's rebirth.

Hope for the children yet to be.
Pray they may find years free from war.
Let us make ploughshares of all swords,
harvesting life healed evermore.

DOUGLAS CLARK, *SOUND THE BAMBOO*
ASIA

Christ the Hope

South – North poles apart
East – West where do you start
      Men are killing – men are laughing
         Baby crying
            Mother sagging
        Youth are shouting
Children hungry
    Women slimming
Dole queue stretching
    Beer flowing
Bombs are sleeping quiet and waiting
      Church is singing
        Jesus weeping
          God is faithful to His people.
Be my eyes to see the suffering
    Love the children – feed their hunger
Be my hands and hold the dying
        Cleanse your ears and hear men speaking
    Strive for Peace – create some laughter
    Teach the young about the Master
      See my father and my mother
hear my sister
    heal my brother
Sow each seed with expectation
    for Mary's child in adoration
    is Christ the Hope of every Nation.

CARYS HUMPHREYS
WALES/TAIWAN

Towards the New Creation

'I have heard what the prophets say, the prophets who speak lies in my name; they cry, "I have had a dream, I have had a dream!" . . . I am against those prophets, says the Lord, who deal in false dreams, and relate them to mislead my people with wild and reckless falsehoods. It was not I who sent them or commissioned them, and they will do this people no good service. This is the word of the Lord' (Jer. 23:25, 32, REB).

Not all dreams are good and true. When we are dreaming, we are entirely alone and at the mercy of our own imaginings. There is no help, no escape from a nightmare. Dreaming – not daydreaming, or visionary dreaming can be a horrible experience, and it is odd that we should use the word as a metaphor for something exciting and good.

The nature of the *dream* is well captured in C. S. Lewis' *The Voyage of the Dawn Treader*. On its long journey of discovery, the ship, the *Dawn Treader*, enters an unnatural darkness. In the darkness comes a man in the extremity of terror, who cries, 'Fly! Fly! About with your ship and fly! Row, row, row for your lives away from this accursed shore . . . This is the island where Dreams come true.'

The sailors interpret not the reality, but the metaphor: 'That's the island I've been looking for this long time,' but the terrified man knows what he is talking about: '"Fools!" said the man . . . "Do you not hear what I say? This is where dreams – dreams, do you understand – come to life. Not daydreams: dreams." There was about half a minute's silence and then, with a great clatter of armour, the crew were tumbling down the main hatch as quick as they could and flinging themselves on the oars to row as they had never rowed before.' (*The Voyage of the Dawn Treader*, C. S. Lewis, 1952, Penguin Books.)

Even as a metaphor, the Dream too soon turns to a nightmare. To be caught up in someone else's dream, the self-centred purpose of a tyrant or a cruel master, the crushing mechanism of a political ideal, must be the worst helplessness of all. This section deals with the great mass of human misery arising from people's dreams, which should never have come to reality, either because they are inherently self-centred and cruel, or because even the best of human ideals are flawed, partial and exclusive.

It begins by waking from sleep: 'Is it morning?' Reality and fearful fantasy are mixed, as the homeless person readjusts to the silent bodies who share the cardboard accommodation. The daylight brings some relief, but the night will come again. It is the night of poverty, the night of injustice, and of helpless victimization, the night shared by Jesus.

Victims are not only individuals. Whole communities are drawn into the struggle. Running through this section is the nightmare of South Africa, and its awakening to a new morning. It is a nightmare shared in part by indigenous people in every country on which the greedy eyes of the European, the *pakeha*, have fallen. Aaron Kramer sings, 'Too long I thirst in shadow, it's time I shared the dawn.' We are invited to acknowledge the ruthless suppression of culture and destruction or enslavement of people. We are invited to share the long night of refugees, driven far from their homes, and the long unequal struggle to live in the face of degradation, unemployment and servitude.

But we are invited to join in the awakening too. India cries out hope, in the challenge of Calcutta, where, 'the courage, the hope, the vision that is generated' make this 'the most exciting city in the world to live in. Calcutta calls for commitment. The uncommitted must look elsewhere.' The Dalit (untouchable) women share with us their marching song, 'To free humanity'.

Other communities give a lead in non-violent reaction to violence suffered, and South Africa invites us to sing, 'Oh God, give us courage to withstand hatred. Oh God, give us courage not to be bitter.'

Ezekiel reminds us that the voice of prophecy is one which calls people to face the reality of the day – to dare to wake from the dream. Josephine Butler 'forced her age to face what most it feared to see, the double standard at the base of its prosperity'. Young people in Mission call us to build a world which emerges from the night. That it is possible is the message of South Africa – the Festival at Crossroads where Festival is possible only through Liberation.

Like the homeless person waking to a brief day, we are all too aware that night will fall again, and the horrors of night are not banished forever. But the promise of the day is there in the hope of resurrection, and in the colours of the sun-shining rainbow coloured cross which leads along the royal road of liberation (Judith Sequoia).

It is necessary to take the night-time darkness seriously. It is profound, and filled with untold human suffering. The darkness is complex. It is hard to find your way through the dark landscape, littered with the interconnected ruins of so many dreams. The only way to the dawn is through the whole extent of the night. But the dawn is there. Shafts of light pierce the night-time in the words of prophets and the actions of liberators.

JANET WOOTTON

DREAM HOME

Shanty House

Is it morning?
Slowly I turn and watch, the
obedient arm move – suddenly
I realize it is mine
the numbness for a time
made it seem it was not a
part of me.
How can I turn
without disturbing these
silent bodies by my sides?
Trapped – confined
Lord, thank you we are only three.

Is it morning?
I jump – noise – voices all around
Is it them, the refuse men?
Listen to their trucks
No – I scream inside my
head – wake up!
Wake up!
They do not move
these silent bodies by my sides
too late, too late
I wait, wait, wait –
Lord, thank you, for it's my mistake.

Is it morning?
How I long to move – bones
so many bones
I lie waiting trying to keep
the pain at bay.
How I long to walk,
just to know my body is still mine.
Gently turn, take comfort from the warmth
trying not to wake these bodies

either side, yet
I yearn for them to speak
Lord, so we can move as one.

It is morning!
I sigh as daylight beckons
through the holes
the night has gone what bliss
Lord, thank you for the dawn!
Awake dear friends
stiff – wet – together
Let's face the day and live
before the night
again enfolds,
with cardboard boxes
with no doors – just holes.

CARYS HUMPHREYS
WALES/TAIWAN

Musical Chairs

How can we judge the poor – and in particular the homeless poor – fairly?

Imagine we are playing a game. A children's game of musical chairs. We've all either played it or watched children playing it. We've made the music for it, and stopped and laughed when someone missed the chair. When there are ten chairs and eleven children, the child who first loses out may be the smallest. Or the most diffident. She may be the one who hates to push, or is slow. He may be frightened by the laughter, confused by the music, inattentive. Or it can be just bad luck. But the problem – if it is a problem – is not the extra child. *The problem is the lack of a chair*.

So it is with homelessness. The problem is the lack of homes.

BARBARA D'ARCY

The Nazarene

I came to this world a stranger
For already my grandparents
Were made strangers in their own land,
It was already decided for me:
Where to be born and what to be fed,
Where to grow up
And what education to have,
It was dark.

I needed something, somebody to hold on to,
I needed something, somebody to make me belong,
I searched everywhere,
I could not find what I wanted,
I tried to create it in my mind
But I failed
Because I am a creature,
It was dark.

Then, the Nazarene saw me weeping,
He spoke to me in my own situation
And he said, 'Child I am on your side,
Who can be against you?'
He identified himself with me,
He became black, poor and oppressed
And black theology was born.

PAKISO TONDI
SOUTH AFRICA

Judgement

With justice he will judge the poor and defend the humble in the land with equity (Isaiah 11:4, REB).

So no place is left for any human pride in the presence of God. By God's act you are in Christ Jesus; . . . in him we have our liberation (1 Corinthians 1:29–30, REB).

He stood before the court in nondescript clothes,
no papers, no fixed address.
The judge cleared his throat,
'Have you anything to say
before I pass sentence?'
What might have been his answer
had the prisoner the gift of speech
and the court the gift of hearing?

'I am condemned because your law
allows no place for me.
My crimes I freely admit:-
I am homeless, seeking shelter
where I may rear my family in modest decency.
I am stateless, seeking country
where I may belong by right in God's good earth.
I am destitute, claiming a share of the wealth
that is our common heritage.
I am a sinner, needing aid from fellow sinners.

'You will dispose of me according to your law,
but you will not so easily dispose of him
who owns me citizen in his kingdom.
He frowns on crimes your law condones;
pride, selfishness and greed,
self-righteousness,
the worship of all things material
and the refusal to acknowledge me as a brother.

'By your law I stand condemned;
but one day you must answer
to the master of us all
for the havoc caused by your law
in his realm.'

EDMUND BANYARD
ENGLAND

Ride upon death chariot

They rode upon
the death chariot
to their Golgotha – three vagrants
whose papers to be in Caesar's empire
were not in order:

The sun
shrivelled their bodies
in the mobile tomb
as airtight as canned fish.

We're hot!
We're thirsty!
We're hungry!

The centurion
touched their tongues
with the tip of a lance
dipped in apathy:

'Don't cry to me
but to Caesar who
crucifies you.'

A woman came to wipe their faces.
She carried a dishcloth
full of bread and tea.
We're dying!

The centurion
washed his hands.

MBUYSENI OSWALD MTSHALI,
1971

Let justice roll down

Let justice roll down like a river
Let justice roll down to the sea
Let justice roll down like a river
Let justice begin through me.

Justice for all who go hungry
crying to God to be fed,
left in a world of abundance
to beg for a morsel of bread.

Justice for those who are homeless,
victims of war or of need,
trapped on the borders of nowhere,
lost in the canyons of greed.

Justice for all who are powerless,
yearning for freedom in vain,
plundered and robbed of their birthright,
silently bearing their pain.

COLIN GIBSON
AOTEAROA NEW ZEALAND

Whose Land? Theology from a cultural outlook

Owura Amu, an educated African Christian, said to my generation that God was in our midst before the white man came. An incident in his life has become a classic example of the lack of sensitivity to African culture on the part of the early carriers of the Christian message.

Owura Amu was once refused the pulpit of the Pres-byterians (then Basel Mission) because he went to his appointment wearing the Ghanaian Toga. I hasten to add that this contempt for African traditional clothing, even when modified by European fashions, was found not only in church but also among the anglicized Ghanaians, especially those on the coast. My mother remembers a lawyer who, seeing his daughter wearing African traditional dress, exploded, 'Off you go and get dressed. I thought you were one of these *adefo* [villagers] who come here to sell *dokon* [a wrapped dumpling of corn dough].'

The African clergy has only recently attempted to adapt African clothing into the liturgical garments of the clergy. After Vatican II African colours and patterns appeared in the stoles of Catholic priests in Nigeria. Rev Margaret Boamah-Secu hallowed the clothes which the Ghanaian lawyer ridiculed by wearing a Roman shirt and collar with an African skirt to celebrate Holy Communion in Ibadan at the closing worship of African women theologians in September 1980.

On the whole, however, it is the Roman Catholic Church, not the Euro-American Protestant churches in Africa which has taken acculturation seriously. Drums have ceased to be symbols of paganism (in the sense of village religion). The making of drums has been secularized. That is, ceremonies that accompany their manufacture have been declared null and void and so ignored by Christians. Of course drums are always especially dedicated in church before being used there, but so is most other church bric-a-brac such as fans and floor carpets. The carved stations of the cross and the church linen can now come direct from Africa. The earth is the Lord's and everything in it too, and on this foundation Christianity is coming to terms with the external manifestations of African culture.

FROM *HEARING AND KNOWING*,
AFRICA

Muka woman

He whakahonore i a Freda

Mindful of the proverb
Handed down from her forebears
Committed to her *whanau*,
At home in Tokerau

Servant of harvest *whaea*,
others before herself,
tirelessly working with diligence
keeping the *whanau* together

Muka in education,
net-working public relations
linking designs to technology
plaiting, *raranga*, *whiriwhiri*

blending old threads with new fibres
weaving new patterns of learning
nourishing, nurturing, *manaaki*
encouraging teachers to try

Muka of the Tiriti
human relationships matter
revealing a light of justice
healing the hurts and pains

Muka of flexible origin
traditional culturally strong
whiringa wahine, whiringa kotiro
whiringa matauranga

Muka from the *korari*
muka from the flax
he aha te mea nui i tenei tau
He wahine, he wahine, he wahine

Nga mihi nui e te whaea – Kia ora Freda

MONA RIINI
AOTEAROA NEW ZEALAND

Do the eyes have it?

At little St Peter's-by-the-Sea, Mokau
I received Communion
from a Maori man,
old, grey, gentle and gracious,
named Rua, a kaumatua.
As he passed the Covenant Cup
for sip of communal Wine
I glanced up, looked deep
into eyes glinting, brown, warm, wise.
Yet I saw more . . .
it seemed
that I penetrated a thousand years
of spiritual Maori lore
crystallised now in Maori worldview
in the eyes of Rua
in which love, acceptance shone
with a glimmer of humour
ignited by wisdom.

And what saw Rua in mine
as I took the Cup
drank deep the Wine?
For my European forebears
have worshipped Christ
since Anglo-Saxon times.

Did divine spark match spark divine?
Did fire match fire?
Was God mirrored there
beyond time, in mine?

GLENN JETTA BARCLAY
AOTEAROA NEW ZEALAND

Is it enough?

Face to face we sit –
the silence, like a stone wall,
separating us.

It is not enough
to sit in proximity
if we have no trust.

Give us hearts of flesh
to grieve our hostility:
then grant us laughter

and let us reach out.
Even if we do not see
eye to eye clearly

dare us open up
our hands, be hospitable:
bare us, soul to soul.

KATE COMPSTON
ENGLAND

Speaking in Monochrome

Our colours were washed out of us
Cane scourged and humiliated
We ached for approval,
Shedding our own definitions
To share uniform meaning
And fade into the chorus
Where our singing was awkward
With slow bleaching tongues.

But we managed, improved by Shakespeare
And all the big names
We were told we'd been done a favour –
(Hobson's choice was our winner)
Swapping our limited means
For those of an empire
We were assured of success
And the voice of the future.

Our bowdlerised remnants stuck behind glass;
Entombed in Tradition,
Consigned to Ye Olde,
Good for a party piece
or light Academia –
An embarrassed status:
what staining still stuck
Kept us in our place.

As the walls around words deconstruct
So our sanitised accents
Proved democracy's truth
By Bow-Belled stock-brokers
And real Wigan Peers;
while the trendy demotic
And authorised argots
Give transient pigment.

Homogenised, all diversity drained,
Wringing wit from the dregs,
Jackdaws scratting
For the mindcatching hues,
Lost in stratified memory
of our translated pasts,
Amorphous and beaten
We sink into grey.

Sailing against the tide with old skills
You lift me from the slate seas
And clear the brine from my eyes
To declare your sunrising
In myriad colour.

JO HANLON
SCOTLAND

Umsebenzi wo mlungu[1]

Sorry my child
I am working
Ndi yenza umsebenzi wo mlungu![2]
Busy making a lot of money for 'Baas'
To enable him to have ostentatious life-style
Last Monday he bought himself a new Merc C.O.D.
This time last year
He bought his family another holiday house
In the plush area of Umhlanga rocks
A third one in the list;
While I have a *Mkhuku*[3] for a home
And every morning I ride an old bicycle to work.

Notes:
[1] The work of a white person
[2] I am working for a white person!
[3] A shack.

Sorry my child
I am working
Ndi yenza umsebenzi wo mlungu!
Ke hlakola[4] 'Missus'
And cook for her husband and children
I cannot help it;
For I am bound to make life easy for her.
Yesterday she bought herself another set of imported
Gold plated cutlery
While I continue to use plastic tablespoon in the back room
I am a sleep-in maid
At my 'Missus' disposal.

Ndi yenza umsebenzi wo mlungu!
My clock-card says in
From sunrise to sunset.
Monday to Sunday
To worship God with all the community of believers
I regard a luxury;
The only time my clock-card says out
Is during Christmas holidays
When I am given an opportunity
To visit my family at Sebayeng.[5]

I am a sleep-in maid
At my 'Baas' disposal,
In the presence of his Kith and kin
I am a Kaffir-maid.
Safe and alone with him
Wanting to help himself
With 'the thing between my thighs'.
He calls me 'Maartjie'
With a different tone.
I am working.
Ndi yenza umsebenzi wo mlungu.

PAKISO TONDI
SOUTH AFRICA

4 Cleaning up her dirt.
5 A rural setting in Pietersburg, Northern Transvaal.

Sunrise to Freedom

This world has been a prison
Too long for me and mine;
It's time the sun were risen,
I mean to see it shine.
One night I dreamt my daughter
Was just as free as you,
And when I woke I taught her
To dream of freedom too.

My veins have nursed your meadow;
My tears have washed your lawn.
Too long I thirst in shadow,
It's time I shared the dawn.
Too long in midnight mining
I've coaxed your fires with coal;
Inside me there's a pining –
It's time I fed my soul.

I dreamt my son was breaking
His bondage, limb from limb;
As soon as I awakened
I taught that dream to him.
This world has been a prison
Too long for me and mine;
It's time the sun were risen –
I mean to make it shine.

AARON KRAMER

Prayer of Thanksgiving on the occasion of the Year of Indigenous People

God our Creator,
we thank you for our indigenous sisters,
their mothers and fathers,
sisters and brothers,
children companions,
and all their ancestors, for Mother Earth
for their living respect
since immemorial times.

We give thanks, God, for our indigenous sisters,
their resistance and courage,
in the endless struggle for life
overcoming centuries of destruction and death.

We give you thanks, God, for our indigenous sisters
their history shared with us,
their wisdom shared with us,
their hope shared with us
making the links of our sisterhood stronger.

We also want to remember, our God,
all sisters around the world:
from north and south,
from west and east,
that they may be moved
by the wind of Ruach, the Spirit,
becoming living instruments
of healing in the world.

Amen.

MARILIA SCHÜLLER

In Exile

We know the songs of Zion from our youth,
But who can make us sing them, speak their truth
And compel from us their secret
In a strange land?

Chorus: By the rivers of Babylon, we listen and remember.
We hang our harps on the willow tree
And the music of our grief is in the silence.

Our children marry as the years slip by.
We must not let the songs of Zion die,
Nor give away their secret
In a strange land

Chorus: By the rivers of Babylon, we listen and remember
. . .

If we forget our roots and destiny,
We lose our faith in our identity,
So our language is our secret
In a strange land

Chorus: By the rivers of Babylon, we listen and remember
. . .

Our preservation and integrity
Must be maintained through our captivity,
And so strictures guard our secret
In a strange land

Chorus: By the rivers of Babylon, we listen and remember
. . .

Our fear of being absorbed makes us severe:
We must be seen and heard or disappear,
For they hold us with our secret
In a strange land

Chorus: By the rivers of Babylon, we listen and remember
. . .

LOIS AINGER

Dream of a bird

You ask me,
what did I dream?
I dreamt I became a bird.
You ask me, why did I
want to become a bird?
I really wanted to
have wings.
You ask me,
why did I want wings?
These wings would
help me fly back to
my country.
You ask me,
why did I want to
go back there?
Because I wanted to find
something I missed.
You ask me,
what do I miss?
I miss the place where
I lived as a child.
You ask me,
What was that place like?
The place was happy,
my family was close together.
You ask me,
what I remember best?
I still remember my
father reading
the newspaper.
You ask me,
why I think of him?
I miss him and I'm sad.
You ask me,
why I am sad?
I'm sad because all

my friends have fathers.
You ask me,
why does this matter?
Because my father
is far away.
I want to fly to him
like a bird.

A VIETNAMESE BOY,
AGE FOURTEEN

Two letters

The two of us were always together: Mentioning me without saying anything about Aida, to be with Aida without at the same time being with me – that was impossible! We were the epitome of a sincere friendship. With whom would I have joked, with whom would I have laughed to tears, whose secrets would I have kept, whose problems would I have listened to had it not been for you. You, my dearest friend.

If you are awake tonight, don't be sad! You and I will be together again. We will once again complain about our teachers and our parents' lack of understanding. We will carry 'animal sacrifices' at Bairam and motley eggs at Easter. We will get ready to go out for a walk in a warm summer evening. We won't be afraid that someone might separate us because you are Moslem and I Serbian. Don't be sad tonight and never weep because of me. I'll come to embrace you and we'll talk and laugh our hearts out, as only we can.

Remember all the nice things we experienced and they will become our future.

Don't cry tonight! I'll come to pick up your smile and I will give you the nicest song in return.

My dear Sanja
I could never have imagined that the two of us would correspond in this way or be separated for such a long time. I miss your mother and your brother, but most of all you. It's

somehow funny here. You are not here and so I sit at home all day long. Going out is no longer as it used to be. I am often with Aida, Alma, Azelma and Larissa. We often think of you wondering how you look, when you will come back to us and whether you still remember us.

Sanja, I wish you could come here at least for an hour to see this cursed homeland of ours. And if only you knew who has left us! Eh, my Sanja, I could write (or even better: tell you) about so many things but I'll save that for another occasion. We will have to endure until our riffraff comes to its senses. I was in your room yesterday; I needed some notebooks from the first year. I couldn't help crying; for it was as if I saw you all around me. I felt even worse when I met your father. When he told me that he was going to leave Tesanj it was as if everything in me had died. When will we see each other? I can't talk about that any more, for it's too painful.

I am sorry for your grandfather: We've had enough losses as it is. No one from our immediate family is missing, but many of our classmates and some of the guys we used to go out with are no longer among us. Samir (Sanela's) and many more like him have been killed.

So long. I wish you happiness in the name of all of us: mother, father, Dzenad, Janet, Adjin, Redza, but also Begzada. She will always remember you. Take care.

Aida, who loves you very much.

If you can't read everything I wrote, don't blame me but the candlelight.

WOMEN IN BLACK
BELGRADE

You and Me

You saw the sun rising from the sea
I saw the sun rising from the mountains
We argued for a long time,
Until you visited me and I visited you.
We saw the different facts.
You say it's summer
I say it's winter
We argued for a long time.
Then you visited me in the South
and I visited you in the North.
We saw the different facts.
You say, 'white is beauty'
I say 'black is beauty'
We argued for a long time.
Then you saw the black forest in my country
And I saw the eternal snow on your mountain peaks.
We agreed that the beauty of white is in its clear brightness
and the beauty of black is in its mysterious darkness.
Sharing – face to face – friends we shall become
You and me.

C. M. KAO
TAIWAN

THE UNEQUAL STRUGGLE TO LIVE

For the Least of These

Brown face with deep wrinkles.
You sell beans
in the light of yellow dusk.

I pass by,
as if I see nothing.

Sugarcane cut into my shoulder,
but no rice for my work.
I am ever hungry.

I pat my mountain belly.
Ah, overeating again, everyday.

There is only
one pair of shoes.
Go to church in rotation.
'Your turn today, my sister.'

I dress up with high heels on.
'Oh God! I praise thee for my wealth.'

Again catchings are
small fish.
Sold for 10 pesos, then
bought some soap.
No more money left.

I sat in front of
roasted fish.
Great fish are
good and cheap.

I am 16.
I have a child.
Police are watching me
behind the door.
'Would you like gogo sir?'

A glass of beer in my hand.
'I pity this girl for
her immorality.'

Your eyes are filled with sorrow,
weeping as if
no more voice.
Stretched arms are seeking for hands.

I sat in my armchair,
slumbering and dreaming
of God's reign.

The Lord said,
'Whenever you do it
for the least of these
you did it unto me.'

ETSUKO YAMADA
ASIA

A Litany for workers

Leader: We come to you our God in strength,
muscles in our arms,
power in our back,
and nimbleness in our fingers.
Thanking you for health.

People: *We've earned our daily meals with our two hands.*

Leader: Hallow our life's brief span,
in our quest for fairer wages,
for security when we grow old,
and an equal share in determining our future.

People: *You've asked us to come to you and put on your yoke,*
and you've promised peace. We come now to you.

Leader:	Remind us always and everyday

Leader: Remind us always and everyday
          that every workshop is a sacred place,
          every struggle a pilgrimage
          and every product made an offering.

People: *You've asked us to take up our cross and follow you,*
          And we follow you.

A GROUP OF ASIAN CHRISTIANS

Worker God

Worker God, who planned creation –
complex splendour held in one;
spoke out threads of light and matter,
weaving what your word had spun,
then, with proper satisfaction,
rested when the work was done.

Who are we to spoil the pattern,
make redundant hands and mind;
tarnish pleasure in achievement
which your pleasure undersigned,
crushing lives, and wasting talent,
uncreating humankind?

Many see the sudden ending
of their deeply cherished plans
through the failure of a system
which no longer meets demands,
and the fruit from years of effort
slips away from helpless hands.

Helplessness fuels bitter anger –
home and loved ones bear the cost.
Voices raised create a Babel,
countermanding Pentecost;
and by this disintegration,
whole communities are lost.

Worker God within creation,
weaving what our hands have spun,
give to us consistent strength
to speak your word and see it done.
So through humble human triumphs
may your victory be won.

JANET H. WOOTTON
ENGLAND

The wise man built his house upon a rock

The wise woman
had no such choice.
Group areas
dictated
her location.

Is wisdom
to be found
in resistance
or collusion?

The wise woman
was a working woman:
domestic labour
away from home.

Is fulfilment
to be found
in resistance
or collusion?

The wise woman
looked after
the dogs
of the white woman's
well secured home.

Is security
to be found
in resistance
or collusion?

And the night came,
and the shadows fell,
and the arsonist
set light to
the wise woman's house:
and it burnt up quickly
because it was very fragile.

Is the future
to be found
in intimidation
or freedom?

The wise woman
bought a blanket
and started again.

JANET LEES
ENGLAND AND SOUTH AFRICA

O Calcutta

O Calcutta fascinates. Visitors come from every part of India and the world to pass judgment. Many come to see a city in the throes of death. They come to be shocked, to revel emotionally in stark poverty, to have their heart-strings plucked, to pity. Calcutta has the strength to bear with them, to chide them gently and to send them away silently. There are other visitors, sensitive and mature who come on a pilgrimage. To them Calcutta reveals a strange face of beauty. It is a beauty which only those who have learnt to love their brothers and sisters can see. For others, blinded by the arrogance of power or wealth or lulled into the somnolence of soft living, the city remains silent. It has no message.

For the beauty of Calcutta lies in its people. A strange people who in spite of severe physical handicaps continue to be passionately concerned with justice. A people in dire economic poverty, the result of generations of exploitation, are yet rich in the spirit to struggle for dignity not only for themselves but for every person.

The struggle is not only to be seen in the long processions, the mass meetings, the vigorous wall poster campaigns or the fever of electioneering. It is to be seen in the great efforts to live a life of dignity on the pavements, deprived of any of the outward forms without which 20th century people find it impossible to exist. It is to be seen in the unobtrusive, yet real local leadership by slum leaders to create just structures for community life. It is to be seen in the devoted and visionary work of government officials battling against impossible odds to create urban conditions which are congenial to a fully human life. The courage, the hope, the vision that is generated in Calcutta by these and others make this the most exciting city in the world to live in. Calcutta calls for commitment. The uncommitted must look elsewhere.

SUFFERING AND HOPE,
CHRISTIAN CONFERENCE OF ASIA

Marching Song of Dalit (outcaste) Women

(*Translated from Hindi.*)

Defying police degradation
Tossing aside tradition
We have come!
Dalit, battered woman, worker, farmer,
We have come!
To end dowry, rape and abused authority;
To stop wife beating and cruelty
We have come!
To wipe out women's suppression;
To remove caste oppression;
To free humanity
In a march we have come!

USED BY ARUNA GNANADASON

WHEN COMMUNITY BREAKS DOWN

Taking the Law into their own Hands

They are not martyrs but brigands and they were burnt alive by the *fokonolona* (villagers) even though they were in the gendarmes' hands. Why didn't they go to court? People said that they had been doing wrong for a long time and it was time for them to 'reap what they had sown'. In April they broke into the sisters' home and stole valuable things and medicines meant for the needy people.

Later on they were caught and put into custody where they acknowledged their misdeeds. But what is striking is what followed. The official gendarmes handed them over to the *fokonolona* who, raising a devilish cry of 'Burn them!', then burnt them alive. Such popular sentences often occur at present. Maybe it is important to think over the reason for such a reaction to crime. The main reason is that the people no longer have faith in the judicial system. Very often criminals sent for trial are released without punishment. So people are taking the law into their own hands.

TRANSLATED FROM A MALAGASY NEWSPAPER

Doing unto others . . . as you would have them do

We are sitting together talking justice. My friend works with indigenous people. It is March 1994, a few weeks after the Chapas Indians have been harassed by the military in January 1994. The army was frustrated. World opinion prevented their leaders from ordering killings of those who had revolted against the government and its oppressive policy towards native peoples. The Zapatista Liberation Army (the Chapas) had captured and condemned to life imprisonment the General of the Mexican Army, Absalom Castellanos, who was also the ex-Governor of the State of Chapas. Recently, the ZLA announced his liberation. They commuted his life sentence, 'so that he may live until his last days with the shame of having received pardon and goodness from those whom he has despoiled, humiliated, robbed and assassinated.' Here is shame in a different context. It is the reversal of expectation, 'My captives release me from my captivity.'

In August 1993 seventy-nine Yanomani Indians were massacred. A French anthropologist who witnessed the event observed the disintegration of tribal ways. Yanomani do not steal. Yet because of the activity of the mining companies traditional hunting land had been expropriated and the people moved. Yanomani warriors had raided the local miners camp, stealing mainly food and utensils. The miners hired assassins from Akri to kill the Yanomani people. The killers came upon a village of women, children and old people. The warriors were away from the village. Seventy-nine women, children and old men were killed. The anthropologist interviewed the warriors after the event. 'Everyone is expecting revenge,' he said, 'What form will it take?'

'There will be no revenge,' came the reply.

'Why?'

'We cannot take revenge on people not worthy to be called enemies.'

The anthropologist concluded, 'There has to be dignity both in the combatant and the enemy. Such genocidal destruction is not part of the psyche of the Yanomani.'

PETER B. PRICE

Descent from the Cross

Joseph, who was from the town of Arimathea, asked Pilate if he could take Jesus' body. (Joseph was a follower of Jesus, but in secret, because he was afraid of the Jewish authorities.) Pilate told him he could have the body, so Joseph went and took it away. Nicodemus, who at first had gone to see Jesus at night, went with Joseph, taking with him about thirty kilograms of spices, a mixture of myrrh and aloes. The two men took Jesus' body and wrapped it in linen with the spices according to the Jewish custom of preparing a body for burial (John 19:38–40).

Nailed to a cross because you would not
compromise your convictions.
Nailed to a cross because you would not
bow down before insolent might.
My Saviour, you were laughed at,
derided, bullied, and spat upon
but with unbroken spirit,
Liberator God, you died.

Many young lives are sacrificed
because they will not bend;
many young people are in prison
for following your lead.
Daily, you are crucified
my Saviour, you are sacrificed
in prison cells and torture rooms
of cruel and ruthless powers.

The promise of resurrection,
the power of hope it holds,
and the vision of a new just order
you proclaimed that first Easter morning.
Therefore, dear Saviour, we can affirm
that although bodies are mutilated and broken,
the spirit refuses submission,
Your voice will never be silenced,
great liberating God.

ARUNA GNANADASON
INDIA

Torture

The shadow of death is never far from truth. This is a sobering thought. Torture chambers are there to process truth into false confessions. Trials are staged to turn truth into lies . . . The power which conquers, dominates and exploits cannot stand the truth. The truth that the rich become richer and the poor poorer, that the human spirit cannot be for ever chained to domination and dictatorship, is so naked that it must be covered by torture. That truth is so true that it must be guarded by the police force. That truth is so eloquent that it must be put to silence. This organised crime against truth defiles humanity, mocks people's tears and defies the power of God's love.

C. S. SONG, *THE TEARS OF LADY MENG*

Siph' Amandla

Siph' amandla N'kosi. Wokungesabi.
Siph' amandla N'kosi. Siyawadinga.

O God, give us power to rip down prisons.
O God, give us power to lift the people.

O God, give us courage to withstand hatred.
O God, give us courage not to be bitter.

O God, give us power and make us fearless.
O God, give us power because we need it.

> FROM *SINGING THE LIVING TRADITION*
> SOUTH AFRICA

Reason to Live

Prerna* (which means 'inspiration' in Hindi) comes from
Chiang Mai-Thailand. She is young, pretty and full of life. Like
other young people, she too has dreams and dreams. She has a
one and a half year old son, Heman (which means 'winter' in
Thai language). She calls him 'Cake' with love and affection!
Cake is her only possession, her only strength.

Cake was born to her in the midst of dark clouds of uncertainty, shattered dreams, and absolute hopelessness. Her
husband, a musician, was then struggling to fight for his life.
He was living with HIV/AIDS. He got the infection by a single
contact outside the marital life. That unfortunate episode
turned their lives into a disaster!

He had began showing the Acquired Immuno-Deficiency
Virus Syndrome (AIDS) and the end was just a matter of time.
It was then she found herself pregnant, carrying a baby boy.
Will her dying husband see their child?

Sadness for Prerna was beyond expression and words. She
found herself in a long never-ending dark tunnel. Will she ever
see the light? Why was God so cruel to her?? What was her
fault??? There were no easy answers!!!

She had learnt all about HIV/AIDS while she was nursing her husband in the hospital and left nothing to chance, but the end was destined, and it happened too soon, even before she could come to terms with the reality.

She knows that she is the next . . . and . . . eventually Cake! But she has learnt to face it, no matter what the future holds for her.

Today with her meagre income through stitching clothes, and making handicrafts (for which she only gets donations), she just manages to look after Cake, and keep herself going.

She is not willing to have Cake tested for HIV/AIDS because she knows that the virus is causing the damage.

She has not confided to her family and/or friends for fear of rejection. She will not be able to face it in any way! She wants to live the remaining time of her life without undue worries and stigma attached, and extend care and whatever little help she can to people living with HIV/AIDS.

All she solicits from the Church and the community is to show a little empathy, love, caring, respect and above all sensitivity to help her and other people with AIDS to live a little longer.

*The name Prerna is given to the subject to keep her identity secret.

HAROLD WILLIAMS
ASIA

Dying of loneliness

Dying of loneliness, lost without comfort,
Bearing the stresses that life has to give;
Walking in silence, I've no conversation,
Searching in vain for a reason to live.

Join me in solitude, sit down beside me,
Lord, show compassion, bring pardon and peace;
Value my friendship and give my life purpose,
Chains of my sorrow come break and release.

Bless me with joyfulness, shine in my darkness,
Lead me from sorrow out into the light;
Give me new freedom and hope for tomorrow,
Wings of an eagle to soar on love's flight!

(Tune: 'Stewardship'.)

ANDREW PRATT
ENGLAND

The Beef Show

Glittering dress, neon lights,
Loud music – then I see you
With open mouth that does not sing
With eyes that look but do not see
With hands that move but do not give
With feet that lift but do not dance
Old woman in a child's body
Where is your soul?

*　*　*

How do you cope in your life of captivity?
When did you last know what
it means to live?
Tonight I saw your body, the beauty of creation
but more than that I saw

your eyes – and tried
to see your soul.
What I saw was a nothingness,
a dead soul, unhappiness and fear
– a captive slave
who sang and danced
Whilst I? Watched on feeling
almost nothing – until the anger,
the sadness and dare I confess,
the hopelessness.
Forgive me for giving up on you
but I really did not know what
I could do to ease your
pain, your sorrow.
If only I could have simply reached out
and told you I care.
As a woman I like to
think I understood a little
of your misery – yet what did I do?
I walked away
to the safe, secure world I know.
Forgive me for turning from you
Even though I care.

CARYS HUMPHREYS
WALES/TAIWAN

Note: 'Beef-Show' is a literal translation of a Chinese expression for a strip show. Some 'beef shows' in Taiwan are part of the sex industry which exploits innocent teenagers and young women, both local as well as migrant workers.

For God's sake let us dare

For God's sake let us dare
To pray like Josephine,
Who felt with Christ the world's despair
And asked what love could mean.

He was her truth, her way,
Through her he spoke again
For each exploited Maggie May,
Each modern Magdalen.

She forced her age to face
What most it feared to see,
The double standards at the base
Of its prosperity.

Grant us, like her, no rest
In systems which degrade
At once oppressors and oppressed,
By grace for glory made.

ELIZABETH COSNETT

Note: Josephine Butler (1828–1906, neé Grey) is included in the *Alternative Service Book* of the Church of England (1980) for commemoration as a 'Social Reformer'. The text alludes to her work, but does not tell her story.

She was a native of Northumberland, but is most remembered for her work in Liverpool. Her only daughter died in early childhood in a tragic accident. Josephine found comfort in serving those more unhappy than herself, particularly the prostitutes on the streets of Liverpool and in the workhouse. Despite the diseases rife among them she cared for them first in her own home and then by establishing a refuge.

She shocked her contemporaries by declaring that the guilty ones were not those women but their male clients, and all who perpetuated the view that what was condoned in men could not be condoned in women. She risked her own reputation by campaigning on their behalf, in particular against the humiliating Contagious Diseases Act. The work she began is still influential and is continued by the Josephine Butler Educational Trust and the Josephine Butler Society.

She was sustained in her work by her deep religious faith and a life of prayer.

Love Spoiled

'God is our Father' –
What does it mean,
    when parents desert or
    damage their children?
Help us make sense of the dream.

'Christ is the Bridegroom' –
What does it mean,
    when marriage is ending
    in sharp disillusion?
Help us make sense of the dream.

'Love one another' –
What does it mean,
    when love leads to chaos,
    despair and frustration?
Help us make sense of the dream.

'We are God's image' –
What does it mean,
    when prejudice rules, and
    hatred divides us?
Help us make sense of the dream.

JANET H. WOOTTON
ENGLAND

MAKING SENSE OF THE DREAM?

Cry for World Misery

CWM stands for the Council for World Mission, but it can also mean Cry for World Misery.

Violence is covering the world;
abuse, injuries,
murders, wars,
and brutal massacres.

Drugs are destroying
bodies, minds, spirits,
and human dignity.

People are suffering from
AIDS, cancer,
loneliness, traffic accidents
sex immorality
pollution, starvation,
injustice, oppression
and all sorts of sins.

Oh! Cry! Heavens and earth,
Cry! Sun, moon and stars,
Cry! All creatures!

God! Almighty God!
Grant us
new vision, new strength,
and new hearts.

Enable us
to build a world
which is filled with
Your love, justice
and salvation.

A-Men!

C. M. KAO
TAIWAN

TIM

TIM stands for Training in Mission, which offers young people from CWM partner churches a year of training and experience in different parts of the world.

They say the young are unmotivated,
layabouts, addicted to drugs.
Some may be so
but others sing a different song.

These young people are ready to cross continents
to train in mission.
How varied they are;
some dressed in saris or kangas; some in suits or dresses;
others in jeans and sweaters.
They gladly give a precious year of life,
leaving home and family
to follow Jesus.

It is not an easy year;
it calls for sacrifice.
They encounter different cultures,
wrestle with strange and new ideas;
their minds are stretched,
their bodies are often tired.
They experience mission in action
in a local church.
These are missionaries for today;
timely in their readiness to offer
talents and gifts in the work of God's kingdom.

In them idealism and realism
are joined in commitment to Christ,
the guide and inspiration
in our adventure of faith.
So they return to their varied countries,
eager to reap the harvest from so many seeds sown
in this year of training, learning and growing.

JOHN JOHANSEN-BERG
ENGLAND

Ah, we are murderer

The Sunday school lesson was about Jesus' crucifixion one day. The Sunday school teacher explained the pain that Jesus endured and all the children felt so sad. Then the teacher continued to explain and she said: 'If we continue to do something wrong, we will kill Jesus, it is the same if we do not love our friends and neighbours like ourselves.'

When Nivo, one of the Sunday school members, arrived at home, she said to her mother:

'Mother, we are still murderers.'

Her mother was very surprised and said:

'What did you say? Why are we murderers?'

'Our Sunday school teacher taught us today that if we do not love our neighbours like us, we will kill Jesus, then we are murderers!'

'Who is our neighbour that we did not love?' her mother asked.

'Soa our servant,' her daughter replied, 'because we did not allow her to go to church today, and moreover you talked hardly to her this morning.'

Nivo's mother did not reply and she remembered Jesus' words, 'Whenever you did this for one of the least important of these brothers of mine, you did it for me.'

PERLINE RASOANIRINA
MADAGASCAR

Forgive

Forgive, forgive us, holy God!
Your children call on you to hear!
Our blood is on each other's hands,
we die from hunger, lies and fear.

Forgive us that our souls are numb
to scenes of terror, screams of pain;
that while we pray 'Your kingdom come'
our world is still a battle plain.

Forgive the minds no longer shocked
by homeless poor, by lives abused,
forgive us that the Earth is stacked
with weapons waiting to be used.

Forgive us that our household gods
are self and safety, private need,
forgive us all our fitful prayers:
the token gift, the token deed.

Give us this day the bread of peace,
the hands to share a common good,
the hearts to ache for justice's sake,
the will to stand where Jesus stood.

SHIRLEY ERENA MURRAY
AOTEAROA NEW ZEALAND

Then I saw a new heaven and a new earth

Then I saw a new heaven
and a new earth.
The first heaven
and the first earth
had gone.
No longer
'pie in the sky'
for the oppressed of the earth.
Heaven and earth
had come together
here
and
now.
They were no longer
separated.
I saw the city,
Egoli:
place of gold,
polished and
shining brightly.
And I heard a voice say:
'We are free at last'.
God has answered us,
making a home with us.
No more Group Areas:
black and white
live together.
And God
lives among us,
wiping away our tears.
No more deaths;
women will not weep over the dead,
children will not cry as orphans,
men will not abuse power:
those things are done with.
For all things are being made new.

The constitution
is being re-written
by the people.
The one who is
the beginning
and end
has made our stories
one.
We were thirsty for justice,
but even in deep trouble
hope sprung up in us.
Now it has bubbled over.
We have received
what our ancestors
lived
and
died
for.
We are all children of the Living One
forever.

JANET LEES
ENGLAND/SOUTH AFRICA

A Song of Light

May the anger of Christ be mine,
when the world grows hard and greedy;
when the rich have no care for the poor,
when the powerful take from the needy.

In a world of restless change
standing for love and faith and justice;
in a dark, confusing time bearing light,
the shining light of Christ.

May the pity of Christ be mine,
when the outstretched hand's not taken,
when the jobless stand in line,
when the lonely live forsaken.

In a world of restless change
standing for love and faith and justice;
in a dark, confusing time bearing light,
the shining light of Christ.

May the love of Christ be mine
for the anguished, for the ailing,
for the frail disabled life,
for the fallen, for the failing.

In a world of restless change
standing for love and faith and justice;
in a dark, confusing time bearing light,
the shining light of Christ.

May the actions of Christ be mine,
bringing hope, bringing new direction;
making peace in a warring time,
offering welcome, not rejection.

In a world of restless change
standing for love and faith and justice;
in a dark, confusing time bearing light,
the shining light of Christ.

COLIN GIBSON
AOTEAROA NEW ZEALAND

Festival at Crossroads

(Two speakers: Festival (in Roman type), *Liberation* (in Italic type) and ***both together*** (in bold italic type). You may also like to use the mime described in the footnotes.)

Festival *and liberation* ***are linked.***[1]

How can we celebrate *when people are oppressed simply because they are black?*[2]

How can we celebrate *when people kill each other because of political or religious differences?*

How can we celebrate *when hunger takes its toll of children week by week?*

How can we celebrate *when tribal conflict makes the rivers red with blood?*

In such circumstances a festival is a mockery.[3]

But when the day of liberation comes, then there is a celebration.[4]

It was so when in South Africa the day of the election dawned and all the people of whatever colour or race shared in electing a multi-racial government.

Then there was dancing and music not only in Pretoria, Capetown, Durban and Crossroads but in towns and cities across the world.

So will it be when we overcome the ancient enemies, hunger and disease, as we learn to care for one another sacrificially.[5]

Liberation comes in this way to communities but it is also needed by

[1] Two figures, one dressed in festive garments (Festival) and the other in casual clothes (Liberation) come in from either side and link arms.
[2] Liberation disengages, and moves further away at each of the next four sentences, leaving Festival desolate.
[3] Liberation points at Festival; Festival hangs his/her head.
[4] Liberation runs back and lifts Festival's head up. They dance.
[5] Linking arms again, both lean forward and gaze around the audience – offering the challenge.

individuals. We can be enslaved by our own weakness, ambition or greed. Then we too need liberation.[6]

Jesus teaches that when even a single person finds new life by turning back to God there is joy in heaven.[7]

So it is when each individual experiences liberation; when anyone finds new life in Christ; when the shackles of selfishness and power-seeking are broken.

Then there is a Festival in heaven and on earth.[8]

This liberation is at the heart of all mission which is true to the gospel. This is the good news which replaces despair with hope. This is the celebration evangelism when Christians join together ecumenically to proclaim liberation to the oppressed, healing for the sick and good news to the poor.[9]

Then there is dancing at the crossroads of life.

In such a Festival of Faith there is dynamite as barriers are removed and the people who walked in darkness see a great light.[10]

JOHN JOHANSEN-BERG
ENGLAND

[6] Their gaze alights on a member of the congregation who is in a position of utter desolation (head in hands).
[7] Liberation raises the person's head up (mirroring the action at [1]).
[8] The three dance, then return to the congregation each to pick up another person.
[9] Now all six, or as many as possible, are dancing.
[10] The dancers form a procession and dance together out of the scene.

My Cross

My cross is a rainbow coloured cross,
Violet, Indigo, Blue, Green, Yellow, Orange, Red,
Colours of the rainbow,
A rainbow showed centuries ago to Noah
In a promise never to destroy life again
In a promise fulfilled two thousand years ago.
Redeeming humankind
On the cross.

My cross is a rainbow coloured cross
To liberate all,
North and South, East and West,
Black and White, Yellow and Brown.
Male and Female.

My cross is a rainbow coloured cross,
For I am blue with the pain of oppression
And blue with the struggle for freedom
And green with hope.

As I walk the royal (violet) road of liberation
With flowers yellow, orange and red,
Springing up in celebration,
Of new life
Creating a new Spring,
Of eternal liberation
In the Resurrection of Christ.

JUDITH SEQUEIRA
INDIA

May the God who dances in creation,
who embraces us with human love,
who shakes our lives like thunder,
bless us and drive us out with power
to fill the world with her justice.
Amen.

JANET MORLEY
ENGLAND

PART FIVE

Celebrating the Dream
Creative arts, rituals
and festivals

In this section, human creativity as a force for change is explored through hymns, prayers, drawings, liturgies, dance, origami . . . and other media. After an initial celebration of the urge towards artistic expression and ritual-making, creativity is considered under three headings:

Playfulness, in which our dreams and longings place question marks against the status quo.

Protest, in which our challenge of the powers-that-be may function as the prophetic voice – a voice raised with passion and anger against injustice.

Action for change, in which the harnessing of dream and protest occurs, and there is a determined move into living differently – becoming 'parables of the kingdom'.

HUMAN IMAGINATION AND CREATIVITY

Many of us have experience of a church that has called us to repent, to be obedient, forgive, serve, love, and to evangelize – but rarely to be creative. And yet . . . our being made in the image of God means that we have imagination and are intended to affirm, develop and use it to the full. The Bible calls us to be co-creators with God: it's surely no accident that the Hebrew creation myth has God giving us a garden to till and cultivate. In partnership, we can image and re-image the world:

we can see new visions, dream new dreams, and then labour to re-create it. Given present-day political polarities, and ecological and nuclear threats, it is particularly urgent that we use our imagination and creativity to work towards those Kingdom priorities that challenge injustice, self-seeking, the profit motive, and the search for scapegoats. In and through all such labour will run the thread of joyful celebration – for creativity is powerfully healing, and Christians are Easter people, people of the 'new birth', a 'people who have begun to awaken' ('Good News/Buenas Nuevas') . . .

KATE COMPSTON

In the beginning was the Creative Energy:
the Creative Energy was with God
and the Creative Energy was God.
It was with God in the beginning.
Through it all things came to be.

MATTHEW FOX

People need to rediscover how to give form to their most urgent feelings, conflicts, yearnings and insights . . . so that they might better understand themselves and others, and become whole people – through gesture, movement, colour, rhythm and sound; in their living, in their loving and in their dying, in their creation of a home, a garden or a relationship.

JAMES ROOSE-EVANS

The Lord's Prayer in Arabic

Across all cultures, the circle represents wholeness and the connectedness of creation: the mandala-like quality of this Arabic version of the Lord's Prayer is visually satisfying and healing. Both simple and complex, it reflects the nature of God, and draws us into acknowledging the centrality of God in the world and in all our living.

YOUR WILL BE DONE

Good News

Buenas Nuevas,
buenas nuevas pa mi pueblo,
el que quiera oir, que oiga,
el que quiera ver, que vea.
Lo que esta pasando en medio
de un pueblo que empieza
a despartar,
lo que esta pasando en medio
de un pueblo,
que empieza a caminar.

Translation:
Good News!
Good news for my people!
Those who wish to hear must open their ears.
Those who wish to see must open their eyes.
To hear what is happening in the hearts
of a people who have begun to awaken,
To see what is happening in the hearts
of a people who have begun to walk together.

IN GOD'S IMAGE
LATIN AMERICA

The Singer and the Song

When long before time and the worlds were begun,
when there was no earth and no sky and no sun,
and all was deep silence and night reigned supreme,
and even our Maker had only a dream . . .

. . . the silence was broken when God sang the Song,
and light pierced the darkness and rhythm began,
and with its first birthcries creation was born,
and creaturely voices sang praise to the morn.

The sounds of the creatures were one with their Lord's.
their harmonies sweet and befitting the Word;
the Singer was pleased as the earth sang the Song,
the choir of the creatures re-echoed it long.

Though, down through the ages, the Song disappeared –
its harmonies broken and almost unheard –
the Singer comes to us to sing it again,
– our-God-is-With-Us in the world now as then.

The Light has returned as it came once before,
the Song of the Lord is our own song once more;
so let us all sing with one heart and one voice
the Song of the Singer in whom we rejoice.

To you, God the Singer, our voices we raise,
to you, Song Incarnate, we give all our praise,
to you, Holy Spirit, our life and our breath,
be glory for ever, through life and through death.

PETER W. A. DAVISON
CANADA

Creative People

Lord, your glory fills the world
and is seen in the life and work of all people.
You are present in the experience
and cultural heritage of all races.
You inspire our use of colour, sound and movement
and the rich resources of the earth.
You made us in your image
and gave us your creative ability.

Thank you, Creator and Provider of all.

Thank you for gifts of communication,
speech and language,
for the art of storytelling,
enabling us to pass on traditions
from one generation to another,
for the gift of writing
and the enrichment of mind
that comes from the literature, poetry and wise sayings
of people of many countries and periods of history.

Thank you, Creator and Provider of all.

Thank you for varieties of sound and rhythm
and the power of music and dance
to make us forget ourselves
and become one with the community.

Thank you, Creator and Provider of all.

Thank you for works of art and architecture,
woodcarvings and sculpture,
beautiful jewellery and ornaments,
and the fashioning and design
of clothes and textiles.

Thank you, Creator and Provider of all.

Thank you for the gift of knowledge
and the development of science,
that we can look through microscopes
at the smallest units of your creation
and discover wonders invisible to the human eye;
for the use of radiation
in the diagnosis and treatment of disease;
for new methods of agriculture
to combat soil erosion, cultivate deserts
and provide food for everyone.

Thank you, Creator and Provider of all.

MAUREEN EDWARDS
ENGLAND

Metaphor and symbol are the main 'tools' of the artistic imagination. When dramatized by the Old Testament prophets and
by Jesus and extended into rituals, they are a powerful expression of our intentions and commitment to action.

KATE COMPSTON

Imaging is a positive thought process which is far from new.
Those who practised it in the land of Israel, were called
prophets, and their images grew out of their own experience
and culture – lions lying down with lambs, little children
playing beside venomous snakes, the coming of God's
kingdom of love on earth . . .

ANN VARMA

Symbolic expression is the way to creative freedom . . . In
contrast to all forms of totalitarianism, the symbol stands for
openness, for pointing towards alternative possibilities, for
readiness to experiment in the hope of gaining a fuller understanding of reality.

F. W. DILLISTONE

A public celebration is a rope-bridge of knotted symbols strung across an abyss. We make our crossings hoping the chasm will echo our festive sounds for a moment, as the bridge begins to sway from the rhythms of our dance.

RONALD GRIMES

On Ritual

In all cultures, ritual is a vital part of everyday life – helping to provide a sense of who we are and how we fit into our various groupings and our larger environment. Rituals, from greeting one another to laying our dead to rest, point beyond the gestures or words we use: there is 'something bigger' at stake, a search for, and discovery of, the holy in the mundane or profane.

In an increasingly materialistic, mobile and mechanistic world, we recognize our need to retain – and perhaps consciously to increase the rituals which connect us to ourselves, marrying body, mind, emotions, spirit – and to our families, our communities, and our fragile planet. Christians feel the need to re-explore their central faith-story, to experience its rich symbolism anew, and to find ways of celebrating its power to transform individuals and society: there is a burgeoning interest in reclaiming rituals and festivals that might have been forgotten – and in creating new occasions for celebration. There is a new interest in, and opportunity for, 'borrowing' from other cultures; Westerners know they have been impoverished by relying mainly on white European/American resources, and are finding fresh ways of experiencing the gospel message by sharing and adapting the symbolism, rituals and festivals of other cultures.

Although symbols and rituals must reflect the experience of the group 'borrowing' or adapting them, many people have found that adapting the insights and practices of other cultures has wonderfully opened up for them elements of experience previously lost or disowned in their own. Also, it has been a valuable way of expressing solidarity with fellow human beings in different parts of the globe.

KATE COMPSTON

Celebration (Psalm 98:4–9)

Leader: Hear our laughter, O Lord.
             Listen to our songs
             and feel our excitement.

Response: **There is laughter, light and colour
             as we gather together preparing
             for special days.**

Leader: There is singing, care and warmth
             as we mark the joys and occasions
             in our lives.

Response: **There is confetti, fire crackers and cake
             as we celebrate as people and communities
             the life you have given us.
             Amen.**

COMMISSION FOR MISSION,
UNITING CHURCH IN AUSTRALIA

Symbolic Action in Worship: Some Suggestions

For small prayer or exploration groups:

Plant seeds – indoors or out – each person expressing his/her faith in, hopes, for, and commitment to, the future.*

Make a prayer in clay. If it seems right, speak about the prayers you have 'modelled'. Share how it felt to use the clay. Was the process itself experienced as praying?*

The Japanese poet, Kenji Miyazawa, suggests that we must embrace pain and burn it as fuel for our journey. Encourage each person to share a disappointment, difficulty or personal wound; then – indoors or out – invest bundles of sticks with these pains: embrace them and carry them to a fireplace or brazier. Burn them. Letting go of the pain, try at the same time to appreciate and internalize the warmth and energy of the flames . . . fuel for the pathway to the future.*

Each person in the circle offers a story, or picture, about a person or incident in another part of the world. Information can be gleaned from personal contact, newspapers, Council for World Mission material, the literature produced by development organizations, etc. Using a ball of wool, weave a 'web of connection and concern' between the storytellers, each of whom will 'stand for' the person or situation they have spoken about. The web will be more effective if people, sensing a connection between the last story and their own, resist going doggedly round the circle, but speak when they feel ready. The web can 'thicken' as connections are made with the experience and stories of the participants themselves – and as members are inspired to pray for those they have learned about.**

Have a basket filled with dried fruit, e.g. apricots, prunes. Take a fruit each – identifying it with a dream or hope that has shrivelled, a potentiality never realized. Share comments and feelings if it seems right. After a time of reflection or repentance, place fruits in a bowl of water. Later the same day, return to find and claim fruits that by now will have swollen. Each make a commitment to restore the shrivelled dreams, the untapped potentialities, and to act on them in future.**

An empty envelope is passed around a circle of people. Invite observations, comments, imaginings, reflections about the envelope . . . its past, its future. Then share thoughts and feelings about the message we ourselves carry in our person (i.e. not only what we say on occasions, but our general attitude, our demeanour, the way we go out to – or retreat from – life, etc.). Are we 'messengers of God'? To whom would we particularly like to address ourselves?**

Read Matthew 14:22–36. Then each share a current personal difficulty. Commit the problems to God, each lighting a floating candle and setting it in a large bowl of water, to symbolize God's power to keep you 'above water', and give you the means to overcome and resolve your problem. Community and world events could be similarly shared.*

For larger groups and congregations:

For Palm Sunday: Gather together some symbols of power. You might focus entirely, perhaps, on kinds of head-dress symbolic of power and authority, borrowing or making some examples. Share ideas about power, the expectations of a powerful Messiah – and also about our own craving for status and authority. After discussion, set on a dais a crown of thorns, with the symbols of power around it on a lower level. Contemplate in silence.*

Easter: Thatching or greening the cross: a bare rustic cross is covered with daffodils or other available flowers and leaves. These may either be provided beforehand and laid at the foot of the cross, or members of the congregation may each bring a bunch and come forward to present it. Two people bind the offered flowers to the cross by means of thin wires, attached previously.

FROM *FESTIVAL SERVICES*,
UNITED REFORMED CHURCH

Focusing on a tree, real or pictured, think about how different forms of life relate to, and depend on, its presence. What hinders and encourages its growth? Why are trees called the 'lungs of the planet'? What implications are there for the way we relate to trees and other life forms? Create a Tree of Life collage – or write a prayer that celebrates the 'all-togetherness' of God's world.***

Find out all you can about AIDS. Invite one or two people who are living with AIDS to come and share their experience. Afterwards, give out red ribbons of solidarity, and invite people to wear them and be prepared to explain them to others.

As an alternative to a candlelight service prior to Christmas, an old Welsh form of service might be adapted – the *plygain* – traditionally held early on Christmas morning, for which people gathered, usually bringing their own specially made candles. Local poets were invited to write new carols for this joyful occasion. Scope here for some communal candle-making, creative writing and carolling.

The Jathra or Pilgrimage Tradition

Jathras, or pilgrimages, are an established part of the Indian religious tradition. Every year devotees travel to special places to hear stories of the gods, to worship and to return with the blessings of the Lord of the temple. In south India, discovering that Christian stories held a great attraction too, the Revd. Anantha Rao introduced a Christian jathra at Dudgaon. The custom has now become part of the Christian calendar, in twenty different centres.

---

* Adapted from *Encompassing Presence*, United Reformed Church Prayer Handbook 1993, by Kate Compston.
** Reproduced or adapted from *Edged with Fire*, United Reformed Church Prayer Handbook 1994, by Kate Compston.
*** Reproduced from *A Restless Hope*, United Reformed Church Prayer Handbook 1995, by Kate Compston.

Every year, just after Christmas, seven village congregations in Sadasivepet prepare for their jathra at the top of a hill nearby. A pilgrimage song is prepared; people practise dramas, folk dances and choruses. At nightfall, with decorated bullock carts, they process through the village, singing, drumming and dancing, reciting bible verses at stops along the way. They reach the hilltop and begin a worship service around a granite cross they planted some years ago.

After the formal part of the service, dance, drama and films go on until day-break. People go home in the morning, returning later for a Holy Communion service when there will also be adult and infant baptisms, confirmations, special thank-offerings. For the children, a programme of bible classes and song competitions take place through the afternoon. Christian people of all ages attend, as do people of other faiths.

CHRISTIAN EDUCATION MOVEMENT
INDIA

Symbols of Transcendence

A novel by Jean Watson, *Balloon Watchers*, tells how Diedre Pining, a sub-ordinary young woman living in a sunless one-room flat in Wellington, finds a circle of people who spend their lunchhours on the City Library lawn gazing up at the balloons each one flies. Gradually she joins in too. For they seem so lively and yet relaxed.

Then slowly things begin to happen. One blank wall of her room, she discovers, is really a sunny view-filled window that has become obscured with junk. Her silent, slinking next-room neighbour comes to her pouring out deep emotional needs – and Diedre finds she can help. She discovers other people too are being lifted and expanded by other 'symbols of transcendence', not that the novel itself ever uses such words . . . Upon another lawn another group is engaged in blowing and watching coloured bubbles.

What a daily expanding world of possibilities hardly grasped: from being a wispy non-person and merely a consumer, Diedre somehow becomes an active life-producer and future-maker. For worship means 'worth-ship' – acts that focus our eyes upon what has most value, realisations that lift us . . .

CROSSLINK
AOTEAROA NEW ZEALAND

Rites of Passage

Rites of passage are a particularly important form of ritual, and intercultural borrowing and adaptation happens quietly all the time. Customs are merely headlined here . . .

Birth/childhood
Naming is important in all societies. The Lakota Sioux Indians give inspirational names to which they hope their children will aspire.

Infants of the Blood Indians of the Blackfoot Federation are raised by elders to the sky, in the hope that the radiance of the sun will guide these new human beings throughout the cycle of their lives. Lifting babies aloft is also common in baptismal and other birth ceremonies.

Amongst very diverse groups (traditional Jews, Balinese Hindus, Kenyan Maasai warriors), the first ritual haircut for boys marks the passage from babyhood to adulthood. In the West, the first locks of both boys and girls are commonly kept by the parents.

The first day at kindergarten or school is often marked by music, marching, flowers, special costumes or gifts: in certain European countries, large, traditionally homemade, decorated cones of sweets are given to these young 'first-timers'.

Initiation/adolescence
In the Russian Orthodox Church, the priest paints catechumens' palms with the sign of the cross in water and oil, the latter being a symbol for fullness of life. Baptism, first communion, confirmation or reception into church membership are rituals common to most Christian communities.

Painting and adorning the body is a common ritual in many societies at the time of puberty: throughout Africa, the colours used in body art and ritual clothing act as codes, red symbolizing blood, the life-force; white symbolizing strength and fertility.

Jewish boys celebrate entry into adult status and responsibilities via the *bar mitzvah* ceremony (and now US Jews have an equivalent ceremony for girls – the *bat mitzvah*).

New bonding/adulthood

There is a great variety of rituals surrounding marriage. Flowers, headdresses, rice, cake, clothes and body adornment all mean something fairly similar in different cultures. Much is made, all over the world, of the crossing of threshholds, out of the old family home, into the new marital home. The Kung of South Africa have a simple but lovely ceremony whereby the parents of bride and groom bring a brand from each family 'hearth', and together start a fire for the new family unit.

There are, in some societies, rituals marking entry into working life – and those who choose a celibate religious life go through rites of initiation into their communities which often employ marriage symbolism. In certain cultures, individuals are chosen or 'called' for an elevated spiritual or healing role, and preparation for this can involve fasting, seclusion and trials of various kinds.

Death/remembrance

Burial and cremation rites have different emphases in different cultures – some relying on lamentation (crying, wailing, breast-beating, smearing ashes, etc.), some on celebration (music, dancing, a party), and many on a mixture of both. Ritual provides a context within which shock and denial, anger and guilt, disorientation, grief and finally acceptance, can be expressed and contained. Watching with the dead often plays a valuable part in the process of saying goodbye.

Meals, music, incense-burning, drumming, processions, the flying of kites, fireworks . . . all these can play their part in rites for the dead, combining elements of remembrance and celebration with the need to separate from, and release, the deceased.

Candles are often burned for the departed: in Hiroshima, on the anniversary of the dropping of the atomic bomb, long pathways of candles are created, and paper lanterns are lit and set adrift on the Metoyasu River at dusk.

KATE COMPSTON

CREATIVITY AS PLAYFULNESS

In play, we exercise the muscles of the imagination, and break through the status-quo, expressing longing for what might be. In Aboriginal culture, the time of the 'Dreaming' is related not only to the past, but to a hoped-for future. This longing for a better, healthier, more just and peaceful tomorrow, is apparent in many of the contributions which follow: the Taiwanese artist, Etan, pictures a more harmonious world where people, finding connection with one another, respect and share each other's joys and sorrows; and the amusing but profoundly serious parable, 'The Table of Justice' presents a similar image. But to find such a harmonious world demands struggle – and struggle is not always immediately rewarded. However, to maintain hope, and to celebrate life even in the midst of suffering (see the litany, 'Singing and Dancing with Brazil', Elizabeth Tapia's liturgy 'arising from our people's struggle', and the stories of Vahinemoea and Sadako) – such celebration is itself a powerful affirmation of faith in God's ultimate 'Dream'. If we still have a playful child within us, suffering does not have the last word: the dream, and the celebration of the dream, is the alchemical agent which can turn base metal to gold . . .

KATE COMPSTON

. . . life's splendour forever lies in wait about each one of us in all its fullness, but veiled from view, deep down, invisible, far off. It is there, though not hostile, not reluctant, not deaf. If you summons it by the right word, by its right name, it will come. This is the essence of magic, which does not create but summons.

SKIP STRICKLAND

We etched animals, people, ourselves inside the rock caves, which we sealed off before the Greeks came. We pressed our hands side by side into the soft clay. We called that immortalising our memory, and laughed. This turned into a touch-fest . . .

CHRISTA WOLF

The poor need not only bread. The poor also need beauty.

MONSIGNOR HILDEBRAND

Bush Potato Dreaming

The basic order and symmetry of most Aboriginal 'dreamings' reflects faith in an 'ordered universe'. However, there is a healthy realism about life in the fact that the symmetry (like Nature's own) is never rigidly geometrical. Reality has some odd shapes, and these contribute to, instead of detracting from, the overall beauty of the life God gives us. The apparently childlike simplicity of 'dreaming' pictures does not mean that they lack profundity: the symbolism is often complex and capable of many layers of meaning.

VICTOR JUPURRULA ROSS

Dreams

Dreams are bright exploding
fireworks expressed in the
corners of our minds.

ABIGAIL LEWIS
ENGLAND

God of our Dreamtimes (Joel 2:28–29)

God of all our Dreamtimes, we bring you our dreams.

You dreamed a new dream in your Eden garden,
lived through a shattered dream in your Gethsemane garden,
experienced a fulfilled dream in your Burial garden.

Through the dreams of your people
you have covenanted, warned, prepared, promised.

Plant your strong Spirit of trust and hope
in our dream gardens, we pray. Amen.

COMMISSION FOR MISSION,
UNITING CHURCH IN AUSTRALIA

Our Day

This is my day
A day of rest
A day of hope
A day of peace and happiness.
This is the day the Lord has made
A day to sing
A day to praise
A day to become one in the Spirit.
This is the day the Lord has made
This is my day
This is your day
This is our day.

DOREEN ALEXANDER
GUYANA

We who bear the Human Name

We who bear the human name are like flowers of the field;
without status, without fame, trampled down and made to yield
unprotected and exposed to the scorching wind that blows.
Let all the world now blossom as a field.

Even Solomon of old (said our Lord, the man of peace)
with his glory and his gold could not match the flowers' grace.
We are weak, but we recall how the mighty men must fall.
Let all the world now blossom as a field.

We are people of the field, crowding Asia's city streets.
We are people called to build a community of peace.
We remember, as we toil, hope is springing from the soil.
Let all the world now blossom as a field.

MASAO TAKENAKA
INDONESIA

We Have Come

We have come from far away in order to arrive at a remote
     destination,
We have left the ravine of death in order to arrive at the top of
     the mountain of life.
When we get to our destination we will organize ourselves.
When we get to that distant point
We will have made a worthy revolution.
We will have upset the table of privilege so that we will be
     welcome to sit and eat.
We want to get there.
We can get there.
We will get there,
in the name of Jesus who has helped us
come all that great distance to arrive at our rightful
     destination.
Amen.

JEAN-BERTRAND ARISTIDE
HAITI

The Table of Justice

Imagine we are sitting round a large table. It has a white cloth on it which reaches to the floor. There is one empty seat for 'the Unseen Guest'. The table is laden with good things to eat. All the best fruits and wines of the world are there too. We're having a good time. We are unaware that under the table there is movement. Occasionally someone from the far side of the table disappears and is replaced, but there are a lot of us around the table and we scarcely notice. Gradually, however, we notice hands reaching out grabbing anything that falls from the table. Occasionally we feel someone grab our feet. Some of us just kick. Others surreptitiously pass the occasional plateful down to reaching hands. We are careful though, for we are afraid of the tables being turned.

Then Jesus comes into the room. We're pleased to see him. We smile, wave and beckon him to the seat for 'the Unseen Guest'. But, to our surprise, and then anger, he ignores us and lifts up the corner of the tablecloth and disappears under the table. Around the table people begin murmuring – 'He can't be the real Christ. He is a false Christ – he is Anti-Christ!' A few brave souls say, 'What's he doing down there?' After a little while, sounds of laughter reach us from under the table. Then songs. Some familiar liberation tunes, 'We shall overcome', 'Kumbaya', 'There is a season'.

A little later, the edge of the cloth is lifted and Jesus, holding the hand of a little child, who is holding the hand of another, who is leading yet others, follow out from under the table. Gradually they form a big circle round the table. They sing, even smile, but don't speak to us. But they do look, even stare. We are aware something is happening here, and we are not sure we can cope with it. The singing ceases, and there is silence. 'They' just look. It is as if they are seeking a response. The food and wine on the table is barely touched. There is in reality plenty, but there simply isn't room around the table. Some of us go and join the circle, but most of us see that as only a gesture. It doesn't really solve the problem.

Then someone from North East Asia, Japanese we think,

speaks. 'Where I come from, tables have short legs, and we sit around on the floor cross-legged.' A carpenter is found. He saws the legs off the table. The cloth which reached to the floor is pulled out and the circumference is great enough for all to sit down. The mighty are down from their seats: the humble and poor are lifted up – just like Mary's Magnificat envisaged it would be.

GUILLERMO COOK
LATIN AMERICA
PETER B. PRICE
ENGLAND

Litany

In the Samba Schools of Carnival, the Brazilians sing and dance of the hardships they live.

Leader: We must let our heart, soul and mind sing and dance a little, not to rid us of our problems and suffering, but to remember and live our faith in balance.

People: *Join us in the celebration, O God.*
Free us to the singing and the dancing.

Leader: Perhaps the harder we work, the more joy we will experience in our celebrations.

People: *You work with us in all the creation.*
Release us to your joy, O God.

Leader: But we can only truly celebrate at the party of all parties, when all have bread, freedom and opportunity – when all live abundantly and fully.

People: *But, even now,*
we celebrate the life in our midst.

Leader: We see women who sort through rubbish for a living, and jump for joy at the discovery of a new pair of shoes . . . at the birth of a new life in a poor community . . . in a shanty town of Rio.

People:	**May we share in their joy.**
Leader:	Along our journeys, we celebrate as we go, marking special occasions, victories, and celebrating along with others. **(The people light small candles and name the points of their hope and celebration.)**
Leader:	Join us in the celebration, O God.
People:	**Free us to the singing and the dancing** **as we name every small sign of your reign.**

COMMISSION FOR MISSION
UNITING CHURCH IN AUSTRALIA

Litany of Words and Action

From a 'Liturgy Arising from our People's Struggle for Life and Wholeness':

Gathering

Ritual of cleansing smoke (to be done communally outside). As people gather, invite them to put dried herbal leaves (avocado, mango, guava leaves, etc.) and dried twigs or branches (prepared in advance) in the centre of the ground. Have someone light a candle and burn incense, and another ring a bell (or use a gong). With the lighted candle, start burning the dried leaves, letting the smoke fill the surrounding air. The people, barefoot if possible, then walk silently around the burning leaves. This is a symbol of cleansing and healing (done reverently in silence as being one with nature).

Celebrate Life and Life's Struggles

Leader:	We come together today to be with each other in the presence of Bathala, our God, Creative Power and Love.
People:	**It is a gift to be alive, it is a joy to be together by God's grace.**
Leader:	We breathe together and struggle together . . .

People:	**Compassionate Power, breathe on us, energize and empower us today.**
Leader:	We cry, we complain, we moan, we dream, we act, we cling to hope.
People:	**God of hope, we embrace your promise of protection and abundant life even as we live in the midst of struggle and pain. Amen.**

Fiesta of Sharing and Solidarity

A basket of fruit is placed centrally, together with flowers.

Leader:	We Filipinos love fiestas. Instead of an elaborate and expensive fiesta, we are going to share in a simple fiesta of fruit, symbolizing our gratitude to Mother Earth, and our sharing and solidarity. I invite each one of you to take a fruit and offer it to someone in the group. Wait until everyone has a share of the fruit. Then together sing the Doxology. Let us eat together, smile at each other, and save the seeds of the fruit to be planted later on.

Blessing of oil. A woman who acts as the *babaylan* or priestess holds a jar of oil and, after blessing it, anoints the forehead of each one in the circle, saying, 'Go, my friend, in peace'.

Passing of peace and positive energies.

ELIZABETH TAPIA
PHILIPPINES

Vahinemoea: The 'Girl Who Dreams'

Last night I sat in my office and cried with a colleague about the death of a girl who dreamed.

During office hours, we talk about nuclear testing and toxic waste dumping in the Pacific. Churches are urged and supported to take action with their governments.

But 12 year old Vahinemoea died before churches and congregations have mobilized enough international pressure to stop the poisoning of the air and waters of her home.

First there were headaches. Vahinemoea was not well.

Nobody said leukaemia. In January 1994, she became very ill. Then, on 1st February, the doctors said she must be rushed to Paris to hospital. Her father had never travelled – no one understood what was happening.

They put her on the plane with oxygen. She had had oxygen before by tubes – but then by mask. It was very painful – she cried and said it burnt inside her chest. When they got to Paris she was rushed to hospital. Her father was with her.

One day later, she was asking her father, 'Why, Daddy? Why?' She pushed the mask away and said, 'Daddy we sing now. We sing.' And she and her father sang 'Jesus loves all the little children.'

That was the last thing she did. Within hours she was only surviving on the respirator.

Her father had to decide whether or not to release his daughter from the machine. As he cried in a strange city, away from their home and community, he blamed himself. He had been working in Moruroa (the French nuclear testing site) when his daughter was conceived. He said, 'I went to get money for my family – but I never knew what I was doing to them – I never meant that this should happen.'

He spoke proudly of his little daughter who had shown him how to love God. He says that if it is God's will we must accept it. But he wonders why she went through the additional trauma of dying isolated in a foreign country in winter. Many questions need to be asked about the death of one more little girl. What are the long term effects of testing on the people around Moruroa? Why bring a child so close to death all the way to Paris? Is her death recorded in statistics gathered about cancer and related disease in the Pacific? Who asks about the other children of workers in the critical area?

Maybe the real questions should be whether or not we are following through strongly enough on these issues? Are churches speaking loudly and clearly on policies of dumping toxic waste? What are we really doing about it?

We can all cry for little Vahinemoea. It isn't enough.

BRENDA FITZPATRICK
PACIFIC

Sadako's peace cranes

Sadako was a little Japanese girl, badly affected by the Hiroshima bomb. She was taken to hospital for treatment. The nurses encouraged her and the other children to accept medication by folding for them origami figures out of the small square medicine wrappers. Sadako's favourite figure was the crane: an old Japanese legend said that anyone who faithfully folded 1,000 cranes would have his or her wish fulfilled.

The little girl began folding the cranes herself: her wish was that she should recover. When she sensed that she would never get better, she changed her wish – praying instead for peace between the nations. To every crane she folded, she whispered, 'I will write peace on your wings and you will fly all over the world.' She had folded between 600 and 700 cranes when she died.

The children of Japan learned of Sadako's wish and they, too, began folding cranes. Every year on 6th August, thousands of paper cranes are suspended from the tower in Hiroshima Peace Park.

KATE COMPSTON

A Candle for Peace

In 1986 a group of American Christians was visiting Russia. After a service in a Russian Orthodox Church, an elderly woman pushed three roubles into the hand of the minister leading the party, Dr Blair Monie, and asked him to buy a candle and light it at his services in his church as a symbol of peace.

When he returned home, Dr Monie duly bought a candle in a glass holder and placed it on the Communion table in the First Presbyterian Church, York, Pennsylvania. This is lit at every service of worship. Later that year, the church decided to buy a supply of candles and holders, inviting members of the congregation to send them to other churches with which they had contact. Two members of that congregation had previously been members of Wylde Green United Reformed Church at Sutton Coldfield, England, and they sent a candle to their former church. Wylde Green URC decided to do likewise . . . and now candles are being sent in all directions.

May that old Russian woman's hope for peace be spread far and wide, as churches in many parts of the world receive these reminders of the vital task of working and praying for peace.

GEOFFREY DUNCAN

I Dream of a Church

I dream of a church that joins in with God's laughing
as she rocks in her rapture, enjoying her art:
she's glad of her world, in its risking and growing:
'tis the child she has borne and holds close to her heart.

I dream of a church that joins in with God's weeping
as she crouches, weighed down by the sorrow she sees:
she cries for the hostile, the cold and no-hoping,
for she bears in herself our despair and dis-ease.

I dream of a church that joins in with God's dancing
as she moves like the wind and the wave and the fire:
a church that can pick up its skirts, pirouetting,
with the steps that can signal God's deepest desire.

I dream of a church that joins in with God's loving
as she bends to embrace the unlovely and lost,
a church that can free, by its sharing and daring,
the imprisoned and poor, and then shoulder the cost.

God, make us a church that joins in with your living,
as you cherish and challenge, rein in and release,
a church that is winsome, impassioned, inspiring;
lioness of your justice and lamb of your peace.

KATE COMPSTON
ENGLAND

CREATIVITY AS PROTEST

Imagination is the tool of the youthful dreamer, the prophet and protester. Used with sensitivity, imagination can dream up effective non-violent measures against oppression. As Edward Bulwer-Lytton suggested, 'the pen is mightier than the sword' – and so also may the paintbrush be – and drama, not to mention simple symbolic actions like tree-hugging in India; 'pointing' in Tamil Nadu; building a wall of small cards in Germany ('Wall of Peace', Christa Schneider); and marching, singing and dancing in Madagascar ('Walls of Jericho', Leonard Rakotondrazaka). As an anonymous Korean woman puts it:

A stone is thrown
into a calm lake
and the stone made waves
spreading, reaching to the far end.

KATE COMPSTON

Every totalitarian regime is frightened by the artist . . . Indeed, poetic imagination is the last way left in which to challenge and conflict the dominant reality.

WALTER BRUEGGEMANN

The prophet stands in the middle of the crowd, but his roots are not in the crowd. He emerges according to broader laws. The future brutally speaks through him.

RAINE MARIA RILKE

. . . it is precisely this freedom of the poetic word which frightens power. The Great Inquisitor condemned the Word to death in order to keep his many words in jail. Inquisitors always condemn the Word to silence . . . soon the demands of power realized that the freedom of the Wind is dangerous, because it blows where and how it wills. So, they tried to domesticate it and flying birds were put inside word-cages:

images became dogmas,
metaphors were transformed into doctrines,
poetry was rewritten as 'confessions',
the pregnant silence before the Void
became demands of understanding . . .

RUBEM ALVES

Faith Has Set Us on a Journey

Faith has set us on a journey
    past the landmarks that we know,
        taking risks with no insurance
            but the Word that tells us 'go!'
Friend or job or home or lover
    we may need to leave behind,
        outworn truths and ways of thinking,
            baggage to the past consigned.

Some are swags of easy conscience
    who with others hitch a ride,
        some are tourist-package Christians,
            dollar-safe, with Book and guide.
There are others on this journey –
    those who long and pray and search,
        heave the stones to free the structures,
            love the Christ and leave the Church.

We are this unlikely people
in the body knit as one,
company of clowns and cripples –
some are wise and some can run.
Prophets are our travel agents,
gospel-makers lay this road:
to the place of peace and promise
faith will take us into God.

SHIRLEY ERENA MURRAY
AOTEAROA NEW ZEALAND

Music and Drama

One of the most popular ways of reaching and motivating the people is through music. As someone has put it: it is a prophecy of what life is to be, the rainbow of promise translated from seeing into hearing. A good song stirs the soul. It lifts the soul high and wings it with sublime desires.

Through village fairs and rural festivals the masses may be attracted to attend musical concerts where a new message may be transmitted to them. There is a new movement in some cities where young poets, with their teams, hold street concerts, street theatre, play and sing their own compositions about the condition of contemporary society, economic, social and political. These performances draw large crowds in cities and towns. This medium can be picked up and adopted for communicating the message. Young poets need to be encouraged to analyse the ills of society and write new songs to awaken the masses.

People's entire attitude to society has to be motivated towards developing a better and healthier social order. The communicator has to help remodel society in accordance with developing a spirit of enlightened responsible self-interest in every person.

MADRAS DIOCESE
SOUTH INDIA

Ikebana: Plant Arrangement

Ikebana is the ancient Japanese art of flower arranging. It really belongs to the Shinto religion. Traditionally, one offers flowers at the altar of a shrine or temple, or in the home in the special place called the *tokonoma*. Here the householder's skill produces through flowers a spirit of harmony which reflects the nature of the world. As a discipline, *ikebana* is a way of developing one's attitude and place in the world.

A number of Japanese Christians have now borrowed this art form to help express their own faith. They see the 'way of the flower' as a means of worshipping God as creator and protector of the whole universe.

There are several strands in Christian belief which make *ikebana* immediately acceptable: belief in God as creator of all things and humankind's responsibility for it (Gen. 1:26); a view that God teaches people about himself through his creation (Matt. 6:28–30); and a reminder of God's ongoing love in the face of change (1 Pet. 1:24–25). Christian *ikebana* has incorporated these themes in its subjects – dealing with human joy, care for others, suffering and the promise of new life.

CHRISTIAN EDUCATION MOVEMENT
ASIA

Tree-hugging

Non-violent symbolic actions are often very powerful as a means of protest and consciousness-raising.

The Chipko (tree-hugging) Movement began in the Himalayas in 1973 – a non-violent means of protesting against the large-scale felling of trees. Its inspiration was the old legend of Amrita Devi and her Boshnoi friends, who died hugging trees, in the attempt to prevent the destruction of their 'sisters and brothers' of the natural world. In 1977, the forestry department planned to fell 640 trees in Tehri Garhwal. At a public meeting, the forestry officer lost his composure and shouted: 'You foolish village women, do you not know what these forests bear? Resin, timber and therefore foreign exchange!' The women replied:

'Yes we know.
What do the forests bear?
Soil, water and pure air,
Soil, water and pure air
are the basis of life.'

The tree-hugging movement has spread all over India and has been successful in preventing the felling of thousands of trees.

KATE COMPSTON

Seedlings

There is a very simple and meaningful practice among the woefully underpaid farm labourers of Tamil Nadu, India.

Rice is the staple food for the people of Tamil Nadu. The seed form of rice with its husk is called paddy. Paddy is cultivated in wet fields. It is first sown thickly in a small plot of land. The seedlings are then transplanted in well spaced rows in another larger field made wet and muddy.

Little girls from the families of those at work, will go to the road and nearby streets with small bunches of seedlings in their hands. They will place them at the feet of the passers-by, and, with the left hand pointing to the fields where the work is in progress will stretch out the right hand and ask for a small donation. Many people will just give a few coins, often cursing the urchins for resorting to begging: the real meaning of this 'begging' has eluded them.

The meaning, however, was made known by one little girl. A passer-by scolded her for taking to begging. She faced him courageously and retorted that she was not a beggar. She asked the man to look at the fields where many women were standing in a bent posture in ankle deep wet mud and were involved in transplanting the seedlings. She then told the man that they were working in order that he could be fed and sustained. Having thus made the man aware of his heavy indebtedness to these people who were so poorly paid, she then demanded with great dignity that he give her a handsome donation . . .

The challenge to remember all the underpaid and unpaid labour with a grateful heart is great – and was indeed the reason behind the practice.

Bread is made of God's gifts in nature – rain, fertility of soil, and seed. But it is also made with human labour. The sweat of toil is a constituent element of bread. Our Lord seems to have wanted people, in the eucharist, to become aware how, in ordinary bread, God and human labour were united in a process of self-giving to sustain life.

DHYANCHAND CARR
INDIA

Wall of Peace

When artist Walter Herrmann ended up on the streets, he refused to lose his creativity along with his home. Instead, he began writing messages on pieces of cardboard to highlight the increasing problem of homelessness in Cologne. He tied the cards together to form a wall. Other people followed his example, adding messages to his. But the city authorities refused to let Herrmann leave his wall of cards up overnight. Undeterred, he took it down at night, then loaded the necessary materials onto his bicycle each morning, and returned to one of Cologne's busiest shopping streets to rebuild the entire wall.

The wall grew in both a physical and symbolic sense with the start of the Gulf War in 1991. Herrmann moved the construction to St. Peter's Gate at Cologne Cathedral where it became known as the Klagemauer für den Frieden, or Wailing Wall for Peace, and was used by anyone who wanted to express their concern about the War.

The Klagemauer now consists of over 30,000 pieces of cardboard bearing messages written by people from all over the world and suspended from lengths of string which are tied to lamp posts. Compiled in a variety of languages, they call for world peace, highlighting the plight of the homeless and campaigning against nationalism with its fundamental hatred of foreigners. New messages are added every day, old cards are removed and preserved and none are thrown away. The Klagemauer has become a famous monument – schools borrow the cards for class discussion, churches have used the messages in their services and there has been extensive media coverage.

Kazuo Soda, one of the 350,000 survivors of the Atom Bomb on Nagasaki in 1945, paid an official visit to Cologne where he praised the Klagemauer as a symbol of the 'protective shield against violence and inhumanity'.

CHRISTA SCHNEIDER
GERMANY

Walls of Jericho

Pastor Razafimahefa has written of the measures adopted by many Malagasy in their 1991 struggle against the oppressive regime of President Ratsiraka. In his book on non-violence in Madagascar, he reports the following: 'The demonstrators had no material strength nor armed force to rely on; they depended solely on the power of God.'

Each demonstration in the non-violent struggle began with Christian worship. People had no hesitation in using words and pictures from the Bible. Thus the capture of the city of Jericho became a symbol representing the ultimate objective. The first 'encirclement of the city' was a mass march around Antananarivo which was to be the initial shock to authority. The following demonstrations, including singing, dancing, and sometimes crowds of around 400,000, were all part of the 'shaking of the walls' theme. Some marches led an alternative minister into the government ministry building; often there was no resistance from ministry employees and the two administrations worked side by side.

At the end of May (1991), the first encirclement of the walls of Jericho ended, but the authorities did not submit. A general strike was called in order to increase pressure. The workers and the people wanted to spread the strike throughout Madagascar. It was late November before the non-violent revolution was acknowledged to have succeeded, though many 'walls' had fallen earlier. Edmond Razafimahefa concludes: 'Madagascar would not have got to its present situation if it had not practised non-violence.' A new constitution was completed and various elections were held, and the new government was set up. Calamities were avoided, particularly the real possibility of civil war.

The big lesson of all this is the need for faith, endurance and unity.

LEONARD RAKOTONDRAZAKA
MADAGASCAR

It can be painful and frightening to go out on a limb as one of God's prophets: there will be forces that try to silence the prophetic voice. A picture by Georg Lemke shows a man claiming the power of God against the influence of juju – but one might equally well see the opposing forces as rampant materialism, narrow nationalism, institutionalized racism or sexism, and so on. Instruments of torture surround the 'voice crying in the wilderness', but these instruments are ultimately powerless against a God who, having risked vulnerability of the most extreme kind, triumphed over evil and death.

FROM *I LIE ON MY MAT AND PRAY*
AFRICA

Take Off Your Shoes

Take off your shoes:
Hear a word that leads to danger.
The ground on which you stand is holy ground;
Sacred the place in which is heard that promise
Where slavery is left behind and freedom found.

Go speak a word:
Challenge lies that mean oppression.
The world in which you live is God's domain;
Lonely the road in which is fought that conflict
Between security and hope that threatens pain.

Come travel on:
Leave a past which wants to bind you.
The place towards which you go is promised land;
Hopeful the way in which is made that journey
Where faithful travellers still form a pilgrim band.

GEOFFREY AINGER
ENGLAND

Note: Dramatically this is the voice of God speaking to Moses from the burning bush. Although the words can all be taken to refer to that situation, they can also be seen as moving out from that and speaking to all situations where God is calling for people to act against oppression. The words can be thought of as addressed to one called to lead, or to the whole people of God making their witness individually or collectively.

While essentially a solo song it could be sung together as mutual encouragement. The words demand discussion to discover those situations in contemporary life in which Christians need to be active.

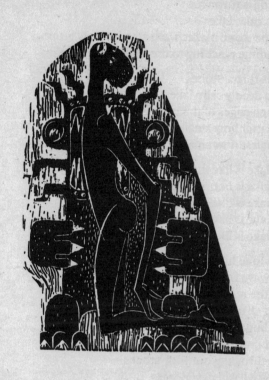

Throwing a Stone in a Calm Lake

A stone is thrown
into a calm lake
and the stone makes waves
spreading, reaching to the far end.

Let us throw stones
into a deadly calm lake
from all edges of the lake
no matter how small is the stone
no matter how small is the wave.

The lake is like the world
The lake is like people's mind
The lake is like sisterhood
The lake is like human bondage
The lake is like chains of oppression

The stone brings awakening
The wave is a movement
And the movement spreads
when all of us
standing together on all sides
around the lake
keep throwing our little stones
The wave will never cease.

Till the whole lake
starts bubbling with life
Till the whole lake
makes its own spring
to keep its own life going.

ANONYMOUS KOREAN WOMAN

CREATIVITY AS ACTION FOR CHANGE

Imagination sees a new day dawning: it makes space for tomorrow to lean into – and shape – today. The mature imagination can say: Let us act *as if* . . . It can make necessary connections, and live out of love – inspired by the vision of peace and justice for the whole of creation. This is living in the light of the Hebrew concept of *shalom*. C. M. Kao and Kate McIlhagga ('The Shadow of the Dove') depict aspects of this – and the idea is taken further in two pieces celebrating the acceptance of people previously marginalized in many societies (David Clark and Witi Ihimaera, 'Companions Let Us Pray Together'). An anticipated death can also be the occasion of deeply moving reconciliations (Mozeshuis Amsterdam, 'AIDS and Saying Goodbye'). Dancing is but one way of celebrating our faith in

. . . one God,
who redeems the waste of all things good,
weaving, from the griefs of our freedom,
new and unhoped-for things;
whose mercy will not fail
to heal all.

SOPHIE CHURCHILL

In co-operative creativity with such a God, joy overcomes despair and change becomes possible as we find our 'angam' in God's abiding presence, and 'go into the world' to 'risk, explore, discover and love'.

KATE COMPSTON

We ordinary people must forge our own beauty. We must set fire to the greyness of our labour with the art of our own lives. In this kind of creation, every day becomes pure enjoyment.

KENJI MIYAZAWA

Give us today the bread of tomorrow . . .

TRANSLATED BY JANET MORLEY

I understand creativity as our power to make connections.

MATTHEW FOX

Sing with your voices, sing with your lips, sing with your lives. The singer himself is the song.

ST AUGUSTINE

Only art as meditation reminds people that the most beautiful thing a potter produces is . . . the potter.

MATTHEW FOX

Dancers

This drawing speaks of the joy we feel when we grasp the possibility of real *metanoia* or change – and begin to live it out.

IN GOD'S IMAGE, ASIA

Prayer in Six Directions

The Ohlone (Native Americans) practise the 'Prayer in Six Directions':

In an unhurried fashion, one greets the six directions in prayer.

We turn to the *east* and face the rising sun. God is praised for the gift of new life, of new days, of youth, of beginnings.

Turning towards the *south*, thanks are given for those people, events and things which warm our lives and help us to grow and develop.

The sun sets in the *west*, and so we praise God for sunsets, nights, for the endings in our lives.

As we face the *north*, we remember the challenges and difficulties in life.

Bending down to touch mother *earth*, we praise the Creator for the things which sustain our lives.

Finally, as we gaze into the *sky*, we thank God for our hopes and dreams.

Centred in the Creator's universe, we remember God's mighty deeds in our lives and can thus move into the future.

MICHAEL GALVIN
USA

The Shadow of the Dove

When dawn's ribbon of glory around the world returns
and the earth emerges from sleep –

May the shadow of the dove be seen,
as she flits across moor and city.
Over the warm breast of the earth she flies,
her shadow falling on the watcher in the tower
the refugee in the ditch,
the weary soldier at the gate.

May the shadow of peace
fall across the all-night sitting of a council,
across the tense negotiators round a table.

May the shadow of hope
be cast across the bars of a hostage cell
filling with momentary light
rooms tense with conflict, bringing a brief respite:
a slither of gold across the dark.

May she fly untiring across flooded fields,
across a city divided by hate and fear,
across a town wreathed in smoke.

May the shadow of reconciliation,
the dove of peace with healing in her wings,
be felt and seen and turned towards
as she makes righteousness shine like the dawn –
the justice of her cause like the noonday sun.

(Psalm 37:6)

Leader: Holy Spirit of love
Response: **Bring healing, bring peace.**

KATE MCILHAGGA
ENGLAND

Spirit of the Living God

This dance was created by Kaneko Machiko for a Japanese dance workshop at the Women's Conference, 1989. 'Spirit of the Living God' was the theme song for the conference.

1. Extend arms at shoulder height, step forward (knees slightly bent) on right foot, sliding it along; slowly shift weight to that foot.
2. Slide left foot forward, even with the right.
3. Step back with right foot; then bring left foot back until it's even.
4. Step back with left foot, then slide right foot back until it's even, arms still extended.
5. Drop arms, step forward on right foot, lifting right arm, palm down, out to the right, about face high. Left arm is bent at elbow, palm up, going across body.
6. Step forward on left foot, bending knee a bit, bringing right arm down across body, palm up. Left arm goes straight out to the side, a little to the back, palm down. (Repeat 5. and 6.)
7. As you turn in a circle, starting on left foot, let right hand come back and, after a graceful wrist twist, put it up by forehead as if shading eyes. Left hand trails behind.
8. Stepping on right foot, with knee bent, lift left foot in prayer, turning a bit facing to the right.

The second time, repeat 1. to 6., then:
7. As in 1., slide right foot forward, arms extended.
8. Bring left foot up past right foot, shifting weight to that foot, while bringing right up behind – almost as if to skip. Meantime, let hands go up toward left, moving them apart a little, as if flower petals are opening.

JUDITH MAY NEWTON AND MAYUMI TABUCHI,
HAIKU, ORIGAMI AND MORE

Angam Day

You're wondering just what significance there is in calling your home partner 'Angam-Partner'?

'Angam' means 'being at home'. The word has the connotations of family, peace, tranquillity, comfort, joy, being at ease, homeliness, sense of completeness, safety and love. It encapsulates the same feeling as when you walk through your front door after a long journey away from home.

For Nauruans, Angam Day will always hold a special place in their lives.

In 1920, an influenza epidemic ravaged the people of Nauru. With an already precarious population of roughly 1,800, it put the survival of the Naurian race seriously at risk. It took over a decade for the population to recover, and in 1932 the Council of Chiefs proclaimed that the day the Nauruan population reached 1,500 would be deemed a public holiday.

The figure 1,500, precarious as it may be, was regarded as a promisingly healthy base for assured re-generation of the Nauruan people. In short, it provided hope for the survival of the Nauruan race.

That hope was achieved on October 26, 1932, when destiny smiled upon baby girl, Eidagaruwo Degidoa. The Nauruan people had come into their 'Angam'.

During World War 2, the Japanese occupied Nauru in August 1942. In the following year, 1,200 Nauruans were deported to Truk, Caroline Islands, to serve as labourers for the Japanese forces there.

Australian forces re-occupied Nauru on 13 September, 1945, and four and a half months later – 31 January 1946 – 737 Nauruans of the 1,200 deported, stepped on Nauru soil again.

The population had dwindled to a little over 1,300. The Nauruans looked ahead to 'Angam' for their race again, using the same target of 1,500.

On 31 March 1947, baby girl, Enparoe Adam, rekindled that Angam hope again.

So you see, your Angam-Partner is one very close to you, and whom you feel very much at Angam with . . .

NAURU, CENTRAL PACIFIC

A Story on the Road to Emmaus

Time: After a Christmas worship. Place: A corner in the worship place. Characters: Three participants in the worship: S (stranger), M (man), W (woman).

S: *(Greets others happily)* Hi! Merry Christmas!

M&W: *(In a dispirited and discouraged tone)* Hi! Merry Christmas.

S: *(With doubt)* Friends, Christmas is a joyful day for the whole world – especially us Christians. Why are you so sad? Please tell me so that I can share your problem.

W: You can't understand. It's difficult to tell.

M: Also there are too many in the world that can't accept this reality.

S: What's so difficult to tell? You don't tell and, of course, nobody can understand. OK, let others misunderstand, but our God won't. God so loved the world that God gave us the only Son. He surely understands what we are.

W: *(With doubt)* Really? Our God really understands?

M: God really accepts me even though I'm gay?

W: What wrong have we done? It is just that our sex preference is different from that of the majority in society, but why are we called abnormal? We are laughed at and even discriminated against.

M: What wrong have we done? The same sex preference is as natural as breathing to us. It's part of our life. If I were forced to change, I don't know whether that person would really be me. I dare not express my true feelings in front of others. Who can understand my inner struggles and loneliness?

S: I think the church can help. The church is the body of Christ and you are part of it. The members will accept you, won't they?

M: My dear friend, you must be a visitor from a foreign country. You don't understand the situation of the local churches. In my church, I'm 'invisible', and they don't know me really. They don't care.

W: We are homosexuals. People in the church are only concerned about how to change us to become like them.

M: Maybe if I were willing to recognize myself as a 'patient', I could remain in the church.

W: Or maybe we could satisfy their demand by changing our sexual preference and they would accept us.

M: But it's impossible.

W: Nor is it reasonable.

M: If we won't change our sexual preference, they advise us to observe celibacy 'for the sake of our Lord', to follow the example of Jesus.

S: Did Jesus ask you to observe celibacy?

W: I don't know. I just feel that celibacy is not my wish, nor can I see its meaning to my life.

M: I'm afraid of loneliness. I need love.

S: Concerning celibacy, Jesus said 'Not all men can receive this saying . . . He who is able to receive this, let him receive it'. They can't force you, can they?

W: They only want to change us. They know nothing about our inner feelings.

M: It seems that if we follow them or not, God won't love us any more. I'm really not sure about God's love. Does Jesus accept us?

S: Didn't our Lord Jesus say that he came not to condemn, nor kill, neither destroy nor oppress? Didn't he come that everyone may have life and have it abundantly and authentically?

W: Everyone? Including us – a group from a powerless minority?

S: Yes, sure. Because God neither shares power with the powerful nor shares wealth with the rich, but he scatters the proud, exalts those of low degree, fills the hungry with good things and strengthens the weak.

M: What you mean is that we, this group of people, can also share the blessing of the Gospel?

S: Didn't Jesus say he would spread the good news to the poor without power, release the captive, free the oppressed, recover sight to the blind and proclaim the acceptable year of the Lord – accepting everyone in society – no matter whether high or low, poor or rich, male or female, master or slave, homosexual or hetero-sexual? Everyone is acceptable to the Lord.

W: Dear friend, thank you for your comfort and encour-agement. However, I have to remind you that you can only say these words here. Don't speak them outside.

M: Otherwise they will expel you!

W: They will treat you as one of us and discriminate against you.

M&W: They will crucify you!

S: I know. Two thousand years ago when I came here, I spoke the same words and did the same things. I have already been vilified and crucified. Now what am I afraid of?

M&W: (*Surprised and doubtful*) Dear friend, who are you?

JOSEPH, SHERRON AND CHRIS
HONG KONG

Companions Let Us Pray Together

Companions let us pray together,
in this place affirm our faith.
God who made us is here among us,
we stand together in God's grace.

> We are *whanau* (family) we are one,
> brothers, sisters of the Son.
> We are reaching for our freedom,
> the prize that Christ has won.

The broken Christ stands here among us,
shares our suffering and our pain.
In breaking bread we find empowerment
to live in *aroha* (love) again.

The risen Christ brings light and laughter,
celebrates the life we share.
The poured out wine of Christ's self-giving
inspires us to reach out and care.

Now let us sing to God who loves us
and accepts us as we are.
Go out from here and live that message,
proclaim our oneness near and far.

DAVID CLARK AND WITI IHIMAERA
AUSTRALIA

AIDS and Saying Goodbye

A remarkable fact is that in the information and discussions about AIDS in the Moses House, the emphasis has increasingly shifted from what the 'experts' have to say to people with AIDS' own experiences. Their stories do not have to be qualified or authenticated by the reflections of doctors, psychologists, ethicists or pastors. People with AIDS learn from each other and increasingly determine what form the last part their lives will take. This is especially true of their last farewell. Old, routine and perhaps timeworn rituals surrounding death are giving way to new, spontaneous and moving forms of saying goodbye and support between the dying and those they leave behind. Parents and friends are explicitly showing their commitment before and after death.

On various occasions in the Moses House, Ria Bos, the mother of Marieke who died of AIDS at a young age, told how her daughter together with the people closest to her arranged her farewell and funeral beforehand. Funeral directors are sometimes receptive to their customers' wishes. For Marieke this was not the case. At that point, she decided to arrange everything herself: having a coffin made; settling on the pallbearers; renting cars, designing and having cards printed. Marieke wanted to be laid out at home and asked for her coffin to be lined with nice, warm flannel and red satin. She also wanted to have everyone write his or her name on white cards which were to be fasted on the inside of the lid before the coffin was shut. Marieke also made the arrangement with 'Dansen bij Jansen' (a well-known discotheque in downtown Amsterdam). Everyone could go there after the funeral. Marieke did not mind people being a little sad, but on the day of her funeral, whatever they did, they should not be sitting at home moping.

Ria Bos indicated that this period was very important: 'Together we made our way to the last farewell. In the week before she died, the door to Marieke's room was regularly closed behind her and someone who came to say goodbye. Marieke was ready to die. She was able to arrange everything herself and say "good-bye" to all of her loved ones. Marieke's

funeral could almost be called a festive occasion. Directed by
her ...'

MOZESHUIS AMSTERDAM
THE NETHERLANDS

Roller of Stones

Roller of Stones,
creator of mists
and mystery;
open me
to your life,
letting your
story shine out
to the world.

Give me hope,
        Living God.
Hope in my hands
        to open doors.
Hope in my eyes
        to see possibilities.
Hope in my heart
        to live by faith:
for it is hope
        that rolls away stones.

JANET LEES
ENGLAND/SOUTH AFRICA

A Trinitarian Creed

We believe in one God,
who gave birth to the cosmos and to us,
creating, out of nothing but his will,
a world of rocks, plants and human longing;
whose eyes will not fail
to cry for it all.

We believe in one God,
who redeems the waste of all things good,
weaving, from the griefs of our freedom,
new and unhoped-for things;
whose mercy will not fail
to heal it all.

We believe in one God,
who lives among all people in all places,
calling us from our despair and sleep
to live out Easter in our generation;
whose love will not fail
to hold us all.

SOPHIE CHURCHILL
ENGLAND

God is Weaving

God is crying.
The tapestry
that she wove with such joy
is mutilated, torn,
made into pieces
its beauty worn apart with violence.

God is crying.
But see!
She is gathering the pieces
to weave something new.

She collects
the pieces from hard work
the aim – to defend
the initiative for peace
the protests against injustice
everything that seems
small and weak
words and deeds given
as sacrifice
in hope,
in belief,
in love.

And see!
She is weaving them together
with the golden threads of joy
to a new tapestry
a creation richer, more beautiful
than the old!

God is weaving
patient, persistent
with a smile
that is shimmering like a rainbow
over her face, striped with tears.
And she invites us

not only to continue
to give her
our works
and our suffering pieces.

But even more –
to sit beside her
at the loom of Jubilee
and weave
together with her
the Tapestry of a New Creation.

M. RIENSTRA, TRANSLATED BY YVONNE DAHLIN
NORTH-EAST ASIA/SWEDEN

Take my Gifts

Take my gifts and let me love you,
God who first of all loved me,
gave me light and food and shelter,
gave me life and set me free,
now because your love has touched me,
I have love to give away,
now the bread of love is rising,
loaves of love to multiply!

Take the fruit that I have gathered
from the tree your Spirit sowed,
harvest of your own compassion,
juice that makes the wine of God,
spiced with humour, laced with laughter –
flavour of the Jesus life,
tang of risk and new adventure,
taste and zest beyond belief.

Take whatever I can offer –
gifts that I have yet to find,
skills that I am slow to sharpen,
talents of the hand and mind,
things made beautiful for others
in the place where I must be:
take my gifts and let me love you,
God who first of all loved me.

SHIRLEY ERENA MURRAY
AOTEAROA NEW ZEALAND

Act of Commitment

We commit ourselves
to join with you, O God
to nurture
the plants and animals,
the elements,
the sacred womb of sea and soil.
We offer you
our ability to create and
our potential to release
people's loving energies
for the benefit of all creation.
We sing with you
the song of the universe!
We dance with you
the dance of life!
We are yours
and you in us are hope
for the renewing of nature
through the healing of the nations.

WORSHIP RESOURCES
FOR ASIA SUNDAY, 1993

Go into the World

Leader: Go into the world:
        Dance, laugh, sing and create.
People: **We go with your encouragement, O God.**

Leader: Go into the world:
        Risk, explore, discover and love.
People: **We go with your encouragement, O God.**

Leader: Go into the world:
        Believe, hope, struggle and remember.
People: **We go with the assurance of your love, O God.**
        Thanks be to God!

COMMISSION FOR MISSION,
UNITING CHURCH IN AUSTRALIA

Index

Acknowledgements

The compiler and publisher acknowledge with thanks permission to reproduce copyright material as listed below:

'A Child', Karl Gaspar.

'A Child asked me', © Janet Lees.

'A civilization ruled', by E. F. Schumacher, quoted from *Future is manageable*, Publisher unknown.

'A dramatic poem', by John Coutts, © Christian Aid.

'A God for all Seasons', © Kate Compston.

'A Journey of Questions', © Edward Cox.

'A Litany for workers', written by a group of Asian Christians.

'A Liturgy for Harvest Thanksgiving', © Pack One of the Worship Resources 1990 of the Conference of Churches in Aotearoa, New Zealand (adapted by the Council for Mission and Ecumenical Co-operation).*

'A Parable', by Jose Marins, © CAFOD (Catholic Fund for Overseas Development).*

'A Plea to Us', © Simon Bound

'A public celebration is a rope-bridge', Ronald Grimes, from *Lifeblood of Public Ritual*, © Scarecrow Press, Inc.*

'A Song of Light', words by Colin Gibson, © 1994 Hope Publishing Co., Carol Stream, IL 60188. All rights reserved.

'A Story on the Road to Emmaus', from meditation material used in Christian worship, co-organized by Hong Kong Women Christian Council and the religious group of the 10% Club on 19 December 1993. Written by Joseph, Sherron and Chris – Hong Kong.*

'A Trinitarian Creed', Sophie Churchill.

'A Woman's Experience', © Conference of European Churches (CEC), 1993.

'Act of Commitment', from *Worship Resources for Asia Sunday,* 1993, © Christian Conference of Asia.

'Affirmation of peace and justice', adapted from a creed from Indonesia. Source untraced, Council for Mission and Ecumenical Co-operation, Aotearoa, New Zealand.*

'Ah, we are murderer', © Perline Rasoanirina, Church of Jesus Christ in Madagascar (FJKM).

'AIDS and Saying Goodbye', © Mozeshuis, Amsterdam.

'All she had to live on', from *Reflections on South Africa*, © Janet Lees.

'An Earth Charter for the Churches', from Justice, Peace, and the Integrity of Creation Working Group of the New Zealand Council for Mission and Ecumenical Co-operation.*

'An Encounter in Jamaica', by Liz Baker, News Share, Council for World Mission.

'An Idle Tale', © Kate Compston.

'And Jesus looking upon him', © Lindsay Reynolds.

'And then all that has divided', © Judy Chicago: Merger Poem from *The Dinner Party*.

'Angam Day', Nauru, Central Pacific.

'Brother Sun', by Catherine Ball, aged 12. Written for a Harvest Festival at Thorpe Hamlet, Norfolk, based on the life of St Francis.

'Cease Fire', © Carys Humphreys, a commissioned missionary of the Presbyterian Church of Wales (PCW), currently serves the Presbyterian Church in Taiwan (PCT) under the auspices of CWM.

'Celebration', Commission for Mission, Uniting Church in Australia.

'Central American Lord's Prayer', shortened version.

'Christ the Hope', © Carys Humphreys, a commissioned missionary of the Presbyterian Church in Taiwan (PCT) under the auspices of CWM.

'Come and show us how', prepared by women students in the Pan-African leadership course, Kitwe, Zambia.

'Come to this Christmas singing!', by Shirley Erena Murray and Colin Gibson. Copyright © 1992 by Hope Publishing Co., Carol Stream IL 60188. All rights reserved.

'Communities of Freedom' extract, by Derek Winter, © Christian Aid.

'Companions Let Us Pray Together', words by David Clark and Witi Ihimaera. Written for the National Gay Christian Conference, 1991 Aotearoa New Zealand.*

'Conflict of Rights', Rev Dr R. J. Eyles, St Columba's Presbyterian Parish, Havelock North, New Zealand.

'Creation Covenant', from *Worship Resources for Asia Sunday 1993*. Published by Christian Conference of Asia. Council for Mission and Ecumenical Co-operation, Aotearoa, New Zealand.

'Creative People', © Maureen Edwards.

'Creator God', CCA Worship 1991, © Christian Conference of Asia.*

'Cry for World Misery', © Rev Dr C. M. Kao, is an ordained minister of the Presbyterian Church in Tawian (PCT) and a former General Secretary of the PCT General Assembly.

'Dancers' (illustration), © In God's Image.*

'Dearest Earth, Our Mother', Bill Wallace, from *Singing the Circle*, Book 1 1990.

'Deforestation', Friends of the Earth.*

'Descent from the Cross', Aruna Gnanadason, © *The Bible through Asian Eyes*, Pace Publishing, New Zealand.*

'Do the eyes have it?', © Rev Glenn Jetta Barclay, Minister of Presbyterian

Church of Aotearoa New Zealand, presently co-Director of the Mission Resource Board.*

'Doing unto others', © Canon Peter B. Price, United Society for the Propagation of the Gospel.

'Domingo Claudio', from *Encounters: Lost Children of Angola.* Produced by Barraclough Carey for Channel Four Television Company, Ltd.*

'Dream of a bird', by a 14-year-old Vietnamese boy.

'Dreams', by Abigail Lewis.

'Dust, Goats and Grandfather Clocks',© Janet Lees.

'Dying of loneliness', © Andrew Pratt, CCBI World AIDS Day 1992.

'Earth', © Kate Compston.

'Earth Credo', by Elizabeth S. Tapia, © In God's Image.*

'Earth Prayer', by Shirley Erena Murray. © 1994 by Hope Publishing Co., Carol Stream, IL 60188. All rights reserved.*

'Environment', Commission for Mission, Uniting Church in Australia.*

'Ever fashioning', © Edmund Banyard, from *Beyond the Known.*

'Every totalitarian regime', © Walter Brueggemann.

'Exodus', Ranjini Rebera, *The Bible through Asian Eyes, Christian Conference of Asia,* © Pace Publishers.*

'Faith Has Set Us on a Journey', words by Shirley Erena Murray, copyright © 1992 by Hope Publishing Co., Carol Stream, IL 60188. All rights reserved.

'Festival at Crossroads', edited version used by permission, © Rev John Johansen-Berg.

'Flowers', Dennis Craig.

'For Between Us', © Bob Warwicker.

'For God's sake let us dare', Elizabeth Cosnett, © 1988 Stainer & Bell Ltd, from *Story Song.*

'For the Least of These', Etsuko Yamada, © In God's Image.*

'Forgive us', words by Shirley Erena Murray, © 1995 by Hope Publishing Co. All rights reserved.

'Four Lousy days per year', an extract from *Sharing the Gospel,* © Mona Riini – Tuhoe Tribe, adviser Maori Education, Auckland, New Zealand.

'From anthropocentrism to bio-centrism', Kwok Pui-lan. Edited version from *Ecology and the Recycling of Christianity.* © *Ecumenical Review,* World Council of Churches.

'Give us today the bread of tomorrow', translated by Janet Morley. *Bread of Tomorrow,* Christian Aid/SPCK.*

'Go into the World', Commission for Mission Uniting Church of Australia.

'God is on the side of the poor', extract from *The Road to Damascus, Kairos and Conversion,* © Catholic Institute of International Relations, London. Published by Catholic Institute of International Relations, and Christian Aid. © The Centre of Concern.*

'God is Weaving', M. Rienstra, translated by Yvonne Dahlin.

'God of Freedom', Shirley Erena Murray, words © 1992 by Hope Publishing Co., Carol Stream, IL 60188. All rights reserved.*

'God of our Dreamtimes', Commission for Mission, Uniting Church of Australia.

'God the Conqueror', Robert Allen Warrior. Reprinted with permission, © 1991 Christianity & Crisis, 537 W 121 Street, New York, NY 10027.

'God who created woman and man', Angela Tilby, © Lavinia Byrne.*

'Goodbye, Mom and Dad', © Harold Williams, Christian Conference of Asia.

'Hail to the Lord's Anointed', James Montgomery (1771–1854).

'Hallo God, is that you?', Rita Dalgleish, © Council for World Mission.

'Hiroshima', Pope John Paul II.

'Holy and Hurt', Kate McIlhagga, Minister – United Reformed Church in the United Kingdom and member of the Iona Community.

'Holy is the soil we walk on,' Edmund Banyard, from *The Maker of Things*, a light hearted cantata for all ages, published by the National Christian Education Council (NCEC).*

'Hope for the Children', *Sound the Bamboo*, 1990, Douglas Clark, © Christian Conference of Asia.

'How can we sing a new song', © Kate Compston.*

'I decided that to be a Christian', Fr Manny Lahoz, (a letter from prison), Christian Conference of Asia.

'I Dream of a Church', © Kate Compston. USA and Canada Words © 1994. Hope Publishing Co., Carol Stream, IL 60188. All rights reserved.*

'I spend much of my days reflecting', © Margaret Schrader, Aotearoa, New Zealand.*

'I understand creativity', reprinted from *Original Blessing* by Matthew Fox, © 1983, Bear & Co. Inc., PO Box 2860, Santa Fe, NM 97504.

'If the Land Could Speak', Kalinga (Philippines).

'Ikebana – Plant Arrangement', Christian Education Movement: Encounters with other Faiths and Cultures. Source: Masao Takenaka, 'Consider the Flowers', Asian Christian Art Association, 1990.*

'Il y a de l'espérance', Hanta Ramakavelo.

'Imaging is a positive thought process', Ann Varma.*

'In Exile', © 1993 Lois Ainger. Reproduced by permission of Stainer & Bell Ltd. and Women in Theology from *Reflecting Praise*.

'In October 1982 young Jews and Christians', Barbara Wood. Reprinted with permission from *Our World, God's World* by Barbara Wood © 1986, published by the Bible Reading Fellowship.

'In our Land', Harold Telemaque.

'In the beginning', reprinted from *Original Blessing* by Matthew Fox. © 1983, Bear & Co. Inc., PO Box 2860, Santa Fe, NM 87504.

'In the garden, on the farms', © Bill Wallace, *Something to Sing About*, 1981.

'In the months before we first left', © James Grote.

'In this dark world of turmoil', © Mona Riini – Tuhoe Tribe. Advisor on Maori Education, Auckland, New Zealand.

'Is it enough?', © Kate Compston.

'It is cold', © Hazel Down.

'. . . it is precisely this freedom', Rubem Alves, *The Poet, the Warrior, the Prophet*, © SCM Press, Ltd. and © Trinity Press International.*

'Judgement', © Edmund Banyard, from *Turn but a Stone*, a collection of meditations and prayers, published by National Christian Education Council

(NCEC).*

'Let justice roll down', words by Colin Gibson, © 1994 Hope Publishing Co., Carol Stream, IL 60188. All rights reserved.

'Life or Death', © Maureen Edwards.

'. . . life's splendour forever', Skip Strickland, from his mimeographed paper, *A Theology and Brief Story of Clowning* from *My Perspective* to be found in *The Poet, The Warrior, The Prophet* by Rubem Alves. © Trinity Press International.

'Litany of Mary of Nazareth', © In God's Image.*

'Litany of Words and Action', from *Liturgy Arising from our People's Struggle*, Elizabeth Tapia, © In God's Image.*

'Lord Speak to Us', © Patricia Preece, The Church of the Cornerstone, Milton Keynes.

'Love', Anna Compston, aged 12.

'Love Spoiled', © Janet H. Wootton, 1993.

'Marching Song of Dalit (outcaste) Women', used by Aruna Gnanadason, World Council of Churches.

'Mary Song', anonymous poen entitled 'Mary Song', from Mariology: A Pakeha Perspective, an unpublished paper from *The Consultation on Asian Women's Theology*, Singapore, November 1989. Quoted by Chung Hyun Kyung in *Struggle to be the Sun Again*, SCM Press Ltd., London 1991 and Orbis Books, Maryknoll 1990.

'May the God who dances', © Janet Morley.*

'Mayan Prayer', Popul Vuh Mayan, *Book of the Dawn of Life*, © In God's Image.

'Meditation of Peace', Popul Vuh Mayan, *Book of the Dawn of Life*, © In God's Image.

'Muka woman', © Mona Riini – Tuhoe Tribe. Advisor Maori Education, Auckland, New Zealand.

'Music and Drama', *NewShare*, Mar/Apr 1993, Council for World Mission.

'Musical Chairs', from *The Trampled Vineyard*, a worship anthology on housing and homelessness, published 1992 by CHAS and UNLEASH.*

'My Cross', Judith Sequeira, © In God's Image.*

'My mother's name is worry', by a 12 year old child in a slum area, from *Reading the Bible as Asian Women*, © Christian Conference of Asia.*

'My Prayer', © Ethel Jenkins.

'New Responsibility', © Kate Compston.

'Not all dreams are good and true . . .' from *The Voyage of the Dawn Treader* © C. S. Lewis, HarperCollins*Publishers*.

'Not ours, O Lord, but yours', Donald Hilton, *A Word in Season,* published by the National Christian Education Council (NCEC).*

'O Calcutta', 'Suffering and Hope' – (adapted), *An Anthology of Asian Writings* © Christian Conference of Asia, 1978.

'O God our Father', © Rev Dr Sione Amanaki Havea, Methodist Church in Tonga. Council for Mission and Ecumenical Co-operation, Aotearoa, New Zealand.*

'O God, Friend of the Poor', © Hazel Down.

'Of Maize and Men', Carlos Castro Saavedra, translated by Peter Wright.

'Of Women and Of Women's Hopes we sing', words by Shirley Erena Murray,

'On Friday afternoon', © James Grote.

'On Ritual', © Kate Compston.

'One World', © Anthony G. Burnham.

'Only art as meditation', reprinted from *Original Blessing*, by Matthew Fox, © 1993, Bear & Co. Inc., PO Box 2860, Santa Fe, NM 87504.

'Our Day', © Doreen Alexander.

'Our Father', Central American Lord's Prayer (shortened version).

'Our Hope', popular liberation song among the Youth Movement in South Korea. Presbyterian Church of Korea Youth Department.*

'Peace', © Rev John Johansen-Berg, leader of the Community for Reconciliation.

'Peace Child', Shirley Erena Murray, words © 1992 by Hope Publishing Co., Carol Stream, IL 60188. All rights reserved.

'Peacemakers?', Susan Jones, *What was it like?* © Published by Joint Board of Christian Education, Melbourne, Australia.

'People-circle', © Etan known as Hsu Chih-Kuang from the Taiwan Aborigine Tribe.

'Prayer for Peace', © Rev John Johansen-Berg, leader of the Community for Reconciliation.

'Prayer for Youth Sunday', Council for Mission and Ecumenical Co-operation, Aotearoa, New Zealand.

'Prayer for Youths', © Omodele Craig.

'Prayer from Korea', from a Liturgy of Korean Church Women United, Korea.

'Prayer in Six Directions', Michael Galvin, from 'Tell me a Story' Healing Life's Wounds' in *The Way*, April 1989. Reprinted by permission of The Editors, *The Way*, Heythrop College (University of London), Kensington Square, London.

'Prayer of a Harassed Mum', © Jo Newham.*

'Prayer of Thanksgiving', © Marilia Schüller.

'Praying for Forgiveness', © Rev John Johansen-Berg, Leader of the Community for Reconciliation.

'Prescription for Development', © Cecil Rajendra.

'Reason to Live', © Harold Williams, Christian Conference of Asia, 1994.

'Reconciliation', © WCC 1983, *Vancouver Assembly Worship Book*, WCC Publications, World Council of Churches, Geneva.

'Remembrance', © Kate Compston.

'Ride upon death chariot', © Mbuyiseni Oswald Mtshali 1971. Reprinted from *Sounds of a Cowhide Drum* by Mbuyiseni Oswald Mtshali (1971), by permission of Oxford University Press.

'Rites of Passage', © Kate Compston.

'Roller of Stones', © Janet Lees.

'Sadness', © Laura Braithwaite.

'Seedlings', Dhyanchand Carr, © Christian Conference of Asia: from 'Patterns of Witness in the Midst of Religious Plurality' in *CCA News*, July/August 1993.

'Self-blessing ritual', adapted from 'Rite of Naming' written by and for Kate Pravera and included in *Women-Church: Theology and Practice of Feminist Liturgical Communities* by Rosemary Radford Ruether. Reprinted in arrangement with HarperSanFrancisco, a division of HarperCollins*Publishers*.

'Shanty House; © Carys Humphreys, a commissioned missionary of the Presbyterian Church of Wales (PCW), currently serves the Presbyterian Church in Taiwan (PCT) under the auspices of CWM.

'Sing to us, Mama', © Fan Yew Teng, *Aliran Monthly*, PO Box 1049, 10830 Pulau Pinang, Malaysia.

'Sing with your voices', St Augustine.

'Singing for our lives', *Reading the Bible as Asian Women*, Christian Conference of Asia, 1987.

'Siph' Amandla', from South Africa, words from South Africa, © 1984 Utryck, Walton Music Corp.

'Sorry my child I am working (Umsebenzi wo mlungu)', © Rev Pakiso Tondi. Used by permission with acknowledgement to Rev Dr Michael Moore for his encouragement.

'Speaking in Monochrome', © Jo Hanlon, Unst Writers' Group, Shetland.

'Spirit of the Living God', from *Haiku, Origami and More: Worship and Study Resources from Japan* by Judith May Newton and Mayumi Tabuchi. © 1991 by Friendship Press, Inc.*

'Stolen Land', words by Bruce Cockburn, © Golden Mountain Music Corporation 1986, from the True North album, *Waiting for a Miracle*.*

'Story of a Mother of Triplets', © Sun Ai Lee Park

'Story of Harriet and the cycling tour', Egbert van der Stouw, The Netherlands.

'Sunrise to Freedom', © Aaron Kramer.

'Symbolic Action in Worship', © Kate Compston.

'Symbolic expression', F. W. Dillistone, *The Power of Symbols*, pp. 5-6, © SCM Press, 1986.

'Symbols of Transcendence', reprinted from Crosslink.*

'Take My Gifts', words by Shirley Erena Murray, © 1992 by Hope Publishing Co., Carol Stream, IL 60188. All rights reserved.*

'Take Off Your Shoes', Geoffrey Ainger, © 1993 Stainer and Bell Ltd. and Methodist Church Division of Education and Youth. From 'Story Song'.

'Taking the Law into their own Hands', translated from a Malagasy Newspaper, *Madagascar Tribune*.

'The apartheid of gender', James P. Grant, UNICEF, United Nations Children Fund.*

'The Beef Show', © Carys Humphreys, a commissioned missionary of the Presbyterian Church of Wales (PCW), currently serves the Presbyterian Church in Taiwan (PCT) under the auspices of CWM.

'The Bible and Economics', © Janet Morley, 'Who Runs the World? Ideas for Worship Leaders', Christian Aid 1994.

'The destruction of the environment', *Signs of the Spirit* by Michael Kinnamon (Ed.) 1991, WCC Publications, World Council of Churches, Geneva.

'The Devil and the Singer', extract from *The Smouldering* and, © Julian Eagle, published by the Catholic Institute for International Relations.*

'The divine presense of the Spirit', *Signs of the Spirit* by Michael Kinnamon (Ed.,), 1991. WCC Publications World Council of Churches, Geneva.

'The Earth is the Lord's', Council for World Mission, Youth in Mission Workcamp in Nauru, Pacific, 1991.

'The forest is our livelihood', *Declaration of the Penan Forest People*, Borneo.

'The Goodness of God's Purpose', Barbara Wood.

'The Grain is Ripe', Shirley Erena Murray. Words © 1992 by Hope Publishing Co., Carol Stream, IL 60188. All rights reserved.

'The Hidden God', Rabindranath Tagore, © Christian Conference of Asia.

'The Jathra or Pilgrimage Tradition', Christian Education Movement: Encounters with Other Faiths and Cultures.*

'The Lord's Prayer', Children's camp (8-14 yrs), North India.

'The Lord's Prayer in Arabic' (illustration), 'Your will be done', © Christian Conference of Asia.

'The Nazarene', © Rev Pakiso Rondi. Used by permission with acknowledgment to Rev Dr Michael Moore for his encouragement.

'The Parable of the Sower', (edited by) Philip and Sally Scharper, *The Gospel in Art by the Peasants of Solentiname* © Orbis Books 1985.

'The poor need not only bread', Monsignor Hildebrand.

'The prophet stands', Raine Maria Rilke, in *The Poet, The Warrior, The Prophet* by Rubem Alves, © Trinity Press International.*

'The season of growth', Donald Hilton, *A Word in Season* published by the National Christian Education Council (NCEC) 1984.*

'The Shadow of the Dove', © Kate McIlhagga, a minister of the United Reformed Church in the United Kingdom and a member of the Iona Community.

'The Singer and the Song', © Peter W. A. Davison.

'The Table of Justice', Guillermo Cook, reported by © Canon Peter B. Price, The United Society for the Propagation of the Gospel.

'The Training in Mission Creed', Tepa, Ed., Chung, Birch, Salmon, Omo, Otto, Naomi, Katiteita, Julie, Sui, John. Training in Mission 1992-3, Council for World Mission.

'The Web of Life', © Kate Compston.

'The Whole Environment', © Philip Jones.

'The wise man built his house upon a rock', © Janet Lees. Written whilst serving the Upper Umgeni Presbyterian Church Howick, Natal through the Presbyterian Church of Southern Africa, the United Reformed Church in the United Kingdom, and the Council for World Mission. Adelaide's house was burnt down in Mpophemeni township on Good Friday night, 1994.

'Then I saw a new heaven and a new earth', © Janet Lees, 1994. Howick, Natal, After the South African elections.

'Theology from a cultural outlook', © 'From Hearing and Knowing', Mercy Amba Oduyoye, Orbis Books.*

'There is a woman who is tired', Betty Thompson, *A Chance to Change*, WCC Publications, 1982 World Council of Churches, Geneva.

'Throwing a Stone in a Calm Lake', anonymous Korean Woman.

'TIM', © Rev John Johansen-Berg, Leader of the Community for Reconciliation.

'To Hunger and Thirst for Justice', Ed de la Torré, *Touching Ground – Taking Root* © Socio-pastoral Institute Manila, published by Catholic Institute for International Relations, London.*

'To Kang Duk Kyung', Ranjini Rebera, © Women's Link published by Women's Concerns, Christian Conference of Asia.*

'To Look at Anything', © John Moffitt.

'Tomorrow is Ours', *Reading the Bible as Asian women*, 1987 © Christian Conference of Asia.*

'Torture', © C. S. Song, *The Tears of Lady Meng*, 1981, WCC Publications World Council of Churches, Geneva.*

'Traditions', Sunga Devasunderam, © Council for World Mission, Face to Face, 1991.

'Tree-Hugging', from *Chipko and Appiko: how the people save the trees*, published by Quaker Peace & Service.*

'Two letters', © Women in Black, Belgrade 1994.

'Vahinemoea, The "Girl Who Dreams"', © Brenda Fitzpatrick, World Council of Churches.

'Vibrations of pile-drivers', from *Becoming Peacemakers* 1992.

'Wall of peace', © Christa Schneider.

'Walls of Jericho', Leonard Rakotondrazaka, Church of Jesus Christ in Madagascar (FJKM).

'Waste', © Stephen Orchard.

'We believe that God', from a *Confession of Faith of the Presbyterian Church in Taiwan*, originally adopted on 10th January 1986.*

'We etched animals', © Christa Wolf from *Cassandra*, Virago Press.*

'We have come', Jean-Bertrand Aristide, *In the Parish of the Poor*, © Orbis Books 1993.

'We ordinary people', © Kenji Miyazawa.

'We who Bear the Human Name', Masao Takenaka, *Your Will be Done*, © Christian Conference of Asia.

'What did you do in South Africa, mummy?', © Janet Lees.

'Who is like Jesus', © Rev Ivaleen Amanna.

'Woman', © Juliet Moriah.

'Women of the Way', © Susan Jones, 23 Mitre Street, Gore, New Zealand.

'Worker God', © Janet H. Wootton 1993, written for Unemployment Sunday, UK.

'You and Me', © Rev Dr C. M. Kao, an ordained minister of the Presbyterian Church in Taiwan (PCT), and a former General Secretary of the PCT General Assembly.

Every effort has been made to obtain permission for the use of the items included in this anthology. In some cases, it has proved impossible to trace copyright ownership and sincere apologies are offered to any inadvertent omissions.

* Used by permission.